CGP

Accrington and Rossendale College
release your potential

Library+

Life in the UK

Complete Study & Practice

Everything you need to pass the
British citizenship test... first time!

Contents

Calendar and Timeline

Practice Tests

Published by CGP

Editors:
Jane Applegarth, Joe Brazier, David Broadbent, Lucy Loveluck, Jane Sawers, Jo Sharrock.

Proofreaders:
Rachel Grocott, Luke von Kotze, Anthony Muller, Holly Poynton, Rebecca Tate.

With thanks to Laura Jakubowski for the copyright research.

ISBN: 978 1 84762 778 0

Groovy website: www.cgpbooks.co.uk
Jolly bits of clipart from CorelDRAW®
Printed by Elanders Ltd, Newcastle upon Tyne.

Photocopying — it's dull, grey and sometimes a bit naughty. Luckily it's dead cheap, easy and quick to order more copies of this book from CGP — just call us on 0870 750 1242. Phew!

Introduction

1) This book includes everything you need to pass the Life in the UK test.

2) The questions in the test are based on the Home Office text *Life in the United Kingdom: A Guide for New Residents* 3rd Edition.

3) The Home Office text is split into 5 chapters: *The values and principles of the UK*; *What is the UK?*; *A long and illustrious history*; *A modern, thriving society*; and *The UK government, the law and your role*. The text is included in full in Chapters 1-5 of this book.

4) Alongside the Home Office text, we've included note boxes which have summaries, explanations and diagrams. They will help you to understand and remember the Home Office text.

5) There are quote marks to show you which parts of this book are from the Home Office text, for example:

    " The Elizabethan period is also remembered for the richness of its poetry and drama, especially the plays and poems of William Shakespeare.

    ### William Shakespeare (1564-1616)

    Shakespeare was born in Stratford-upon-Avon, England. He was a playwright and actor and wrote many poems and plays. His most famous plays include *A Midsummer Night's Dream*, *Hamlet*, *Macbeth* and *Romeo and Juliet*...

    These quote marks show this passage is from the Home Office text ⟶ "

6) The practice tests at the back of this book will give you plenty of practice for the real Life in the UK test. We've included answers for every question, so you can mark your tests and see how you're progressing.

7) You'll find more practice questions on the accompanying CD-ROM. You can create tests based on all of the Home Office text (like the real test), or you can pick the chapters you want to answer questions on.

8) There's a page on the important days in the British calendar (page 147) and a timeline of key dates in British history (pages 148-149).

9) There is also a glossary at the back of the book. It explains words and phrases that are in the Home Office text.

The values and principles of the UK

66 Britain is a fantastic place to live: a modern, thriving society with a long and illustrious history. Our people have been at the heart of the world's political, scientific, industrial and cultural development. We are proud of our record of welcoming new migrants who will add to the diversity and dynamism of our national life.

Applying to become a permanent resident or citizen of the UK is an important decision and commitment. You will be agreeing to accept the responsibilities which go with permanent residence and to respect the laws, values and traditions of the UK. Good citizens are an asset to the UK. We welcome those seeking to make a positive contribution to our society.

Passing the Life in the UK test is part of demonstrating that you are ready to become a permanent migrant to the UK. This handbook is designed to support you in your preparation. It will help you to integrate into society and play a full role in your local community. It will also help ensure that you have a broad general knowledge of the culture, laws and history of the UK. 99

1) Britain welcomes new migrants who will make a positive contribution to British society.

2) To become a UK citizen or a permanent resident, you will need to agree to respect British laws, values and traditions.

3) This book will help you gain a broad knowledge of British culture, laws and history.

The UK has a vibrant society and an impressive history

©iStockphoto.com/tonyduoduo

The values and principles of the UK

❝ British society is founded on fundamental values and principles which all those living in the UK should respect and support. These values are reflected in the responsibilities, rights and privileges of being a British citizen or permanent resident of the UK. They are based on history and traditions and are protected by law, customs and expectations. There is no place in British society for extremism or intolerance.

The fundamental principles of British life include:

- Democracy
- The rule of law
- Individual liberty
- Tolerance of those with different faiths and beliefs
- Participation in community life.

As part of the citizenship ceremony, new citizens pledge to uphold these values. The pledge is:

'I will give my loyalty to the United Kingdom and respect its rights and freedoms. I will uphold its democratic values. I will observe its laws faithfully and fulfil my duties and obligations as a British citizen.'

Flowing from the fundamental principles are **responsibilities and freedoms** which are shared by all those living in the UK and which we expect all residents to respect.

If you wish to be a permanent resident or citizen of the UK, you should:

- respect and obey the law
- respect the rights of others, including their right to their own opinions
- treat others with fairness
- look after yourself and your family
- look after the area in which you live and the environment.

In return, the UK offers:

- freedom of belief and religion
- freedom of speech
- freedom from unfair discrimination
- a right to a fair trial
- a right to join in the election of a government.

Becoming a permanent resident

To apply to become a permanent resident or citizen of the UK, you will need to:

- speak and read English
- have a good understanding of life in the UK.

There are currently (as of January 2013) two ways you can be tested on these requirements:

- Take the Life in the UK test. The questions are written in a way that requires an understanding of the English language at English for Speakers of Other Languages (ESOL) Entry Level 3, so there is no need to take a separate English language test.

  Tip: The questions at the back of this book and on the CD-ROM will give you plenty of practice to help you pass the Life in the UK test.

  People here on work visas, including those on Tier 1 and Tier 2 of the points-based system, normally must pass the Life in the UK test to become permanent residents.

- Pass an ESOL course in English with Citizenship. You will need to take this course if your standard of English is below ESOL Entry Level 3. The course will help you to improve your English and learn more about life in the UK. At the end of the course you will take a test.

Once you have passed one of these tests, you can make an application for permanent residence or British citizenship. The form that you have to complete and the evidence that you need to provide will depend on your personal circumstances. There is a fee for submitting an application, which is different for the various types of application. All of the forms and a list of fees can be found on the UK Border Agency website, www.ukba.homeoffice.gov.uk

From October 2013, the requirements will change. From that date, for settlement or permanent residence, you will need to:

- Pass the Life in the UK test

AND

- Produce acceptable evidence of speaking and listening skills in English at B1 of the Common European Framework of Reference. This is equivalent to ESOL Entry Level 3.

The requirements for citizenship applications may also change in the future. Further details will be published on the UK Border Agency website and you should check the information on that website for current requirements before applying for settlement or citizenship. "

1) British society is based on fundamental values and principles that every UK citizen should respect and support.
2) Extremism or intolerance is not acceptable in the UK.
3) If you want to become a permanent resident or citizen of the UK, you must accept certain responsibilities. For example, you should respect and obey the law.
4) In return, you will receive certain rights and freedoms. For example, freedom of speech.

New British citizens pledge to respect the rights, freedoms and values of the UK

Taking the Life in the UK test

" This handbook will help prepare you for taking the Life in the UK test. The test consists of 24 questions about important aspects of life in the UK. Questions are based on ALL parts of the handbook. The 24 questions will be different for each person taking the test at that test session.

The Life in the UK test is usually taken in English, although special arrangements can be made if you wish to take it in Welsh or Scottish Gaelic.

You can only take the test at a registered and approved Life in the UK test centre. There are about 60 test centres around the UK. You can only book your test online, at www.lifeintheuktest.gov.uk. You should not take your test at any other establishment as the UK Border Agency will only accept certificates from registered test centres. If you live on the Isle of Man or in the Channel Islands, there are different arrangements for taking the Life in the UK test.

When booking your test, read the instructions carefully. Make sure you enter your details correctly. You will need to take some identification and proof of your address with you to the test. If you don't take these, you will not be able to take the test.

How to use this handbook

Everything that you will need to know to pass the Life in the UK test is included in this handbook. The questions will be based on the whole book, including this introduction, so make sure you study the entire book thoroughly. The handbook has been written to ensure that anyone who can read English at ESOL Entry Level 3 or above should have no difficulty with the language.

The glossary at the back of the handbook contains some key words and phrases, which you might find helpful.

Where to find more information

You can find out more information from the following places:

- The UK Border Agency website (www.ukba.homeoffice.gov.uk) for more information about the application process and the forms you will need to complete

- The Life in the UK test website (www.lifeintheuktest.gov.uk) for more information about the test and how to book a place to take one

- Gov.uk (www.gov.uk) for information about ESOL courses and how to find one in your area.

What is the UK?

66 The UK is made up of England, Scotland, Wales and Northern Ireland. The rest of Ireland is an independent country.

The official name of the country is the United Kingdom of Great Britain and Northern Ireland. 'Great Britain' refers only to England, Scotland and Wales, not to Northern Ireland. The words 'Britain', 'British Isles' or 'British', however, are used in this book to refer to everyone in the UK.

There are also several islands which are closely linked with the UK but are not part of it: the Channel Islands and the Isle of Man. These have their own governments and are called 'Crown dependencies'. There are also several British overseas territories in other parts of the world, such as St Helena and the Falkland Islands. They are also linked to the UK but are not a part of it.

The UK is governed by the parliament sitting in Westminster. Scotland, Wales and Northern Ireland also have parliaments or assemblies of their own, with devolved powers in defined areas. 🙹🙹

1) Great Britain means England, Scotland and Wales.

2) The United Kingdom means Great Britain and Northern Ireland.

3) The Isle of Man and the Channel Islands are not part of the UK. They are called Crown dependencies and they have their own governments.

4) Britain also has overseas territories, including St Helena and the Falkland Islands. They are not part of the UK, but they have close links to it.

5) The UK parliament is at Westminster in London.

6) Wales, Scotland and Northern Ireland have their own parliaments or assemblies too (see pages 117-119).

The Houses of Parliament at Westminster are a World Heritage Site

A long and illustrious history

Early Britain

66 The first people to live in Britain were hunter-gatherers, in what we call the Stone Age. For much of the Stone Age, Britain was connected to the continent by a land bridge. People came and went, following the herds of deer and horses which they hunted. Britain only became permanently separated from the continent by the Channel about 10,000 years ago.

The first farmers arrived in Britain 6,000 years ago. The ancestors of these first farmers probably came from south-east Europe. These people built houses, tombs and monuments on the land. One of these monuments, Stonehenge, still stands in what is now the English county of Wiltshire. Stonehenge was probably a special gathering place for seasonal ceremonies. Other Stone Age sites have also survived. Skara Brae on Orkney, off the north coast of Scotland, is the best preserved prehistoric village in northern Europe, and has helped archaeologists to understand more about how people lived near the end of the Stone Age.

Around 4,000 years ago, people learned to make bronze. We call this period the Bronze Age. People lived in roundhouses and buried their dead in tombs called round barrows. The people of the Bronze Age were accomplished metalworkers who made many beautiful objects in bronze and gold, including tools, ornaments and weapons. The Bronze Age was followed by the Iron Age, when people learned how to make weapons and tools out of iron. People still lived in roundhouses, grouped together into larger settlements, and sometimes defended sites called hill forts. A very impressive hill fort can still be seen today at Maiden Castle, in the English county of Dorset. Most people were farmers, craft workers or warriors. The language they spoke was part of the Celtic language family. Similar languages were spoken across Europe in the Iron Age, and related languages are still spoken today in some parts of Wales, Scotland and Ireland. The people of the Iron Age had a sophisticated culture and economy. They made the first coins to be minted in Britain, some inscribed with the names of Iron Age kings. This marks the beginnings of British history. 99

1) In the Stone Age, people in Britain were hunter-gatherers (they got all of their food from wild plants and from hunting animals).

2) Surviving Stone Age sites in Britain include Stonehenge in Wiltshire (England), and Skara Brae on Orkney (Scotland). They are both World Heritage sites.

3) The Bronze Age began around 4,000 years ago, when people learned how to make bronze.

4) After the Bronze Age came the Iron Age, when people learned to make weapons and tools out of iron.

5) The first British coins were made during this period.

An Iron Age hill fort can still be seen at Maiden Castle, in Dorset

The Romans

❝Julius Caesar led a Roman invasion of Britain in 55 BC. This was unsuccessful and for nearly 100 years Britain remained separate from the Roman Empire. In AD 43 the Emperor Claudius led the Roman army in a new invasion. This time, there was resistance from some of the British tribes but the Romans were successful in occupying almost all of Britain. One of the tribal leaders who fought against the Romans was Boudicca, the queen of the Iceni in what is now eastern England. She is still remembered today and there is a statue of her on Westminster Bridge in London, near the Houses of Parliament.

Areas of what is now Scotland were never conquered by the Romans, and the Emperor Hadrian built a wall in the north of England to keep out the Picts (ancestors of the Scottish people). Included in the wall were a number of forts. Parts of Hadrian's Wall, including the forts of Housesteads and Vindolanda, can still be seen. It is a popular area for walkers and is a UNESCO (United Nations Educational, Scientific and Cultural Organization) World Heritage Site.

The Romans remained in Britain for 400 years. They built roads and public buildings, created a structure of law, and introduced new plants and animals. It was during the 3rd and 4th centuries AD that the first Christian communities began to appear in Britain. 🟢🟢

1) Julius Caesar led an unsuccessful invasion of Britain in 55 BC.

2) Emperor Claudius led a successful invasion of Britain in AD 43.

3) Boudicca was a British tribal queen from the east of England who fought against the invading Romans.

4) The Romans built Hadrian's Wall in northern England to keep out the Picts (ancestors of the Scottish people).

5) The Romans stayed in Britain for 400 years.

6) The first Christian communities appeared in Britain in the 3rd and 4th centuries AD.

Vindolanda (right) and Housesteads are forts on Hadrian's Wall

The Anglo-Saxons

🟢🟢 The Roman army left Britain in AD 410 to defend other parts of the Roman Empire and never returned. Britain was again invaded by tribes from northern Europe: the Jutes, the Angles and the Saxons. The languages they spoke are the basis of modern-day English. Battles were fought against these invaders but, by about AD 600, Anglo-Saxon kingdoms were established in Britain. These kingdoms were mainly in what is now England. The burial place of one of the kings was at Sutton Hoo in modern Suffolk. This king was buried with treasure and armour, all placed in a ship which was then covered by a mound of earth. Parts of the west of Britain, including much of what is now Wales, and Scotland, remained free of Anglo-Saxon rule.

The Anglo-Saxons were not Christians when they first came to Britain but, during this period, missionaries came to Britain to preach about Christianity. Missionaries from Ireland spread the religion in the north. The most famous of these were St Patrick, who would become the patron saint of Ireland

(see pages 74-75 for more about patron saints), and St Colum.
a monastery on the island of Iona, off the coast of what is .
St Augustine led missionaries from Rome, who spread Christianity
St Augustine became the first Archbishop of Canterbury (see page 7·
about the Archbishop of Canterbury and the Church in Britain today).

The Vikings

The Vikings came from Denmark and Norway. They first visited Britain in
AD 789 to raid coastal towns and take away goods and slaves. Then, they
began to stay and form their own communities in the east of England and
Scotland. The Anglo-Saxon kingdoms in England united under King Alfred
the Great, who defeated the Vikings. Many of the Viking invaders stayed in
Britain — especially in the east and north of England, in an area known as the
Danelaw (many place names there, such as Grimsby and Scunthorpe, come
from the Viking languages). The Viking settlers mixed with local communities
and some converted to Christianity.

Anglo-Saxon kings continued to rule what is now England, except for a short
period when there were Danish kings. The first of these was Cnut, also called
Canute.

In the north, the threat of attack by Vikings had encouraged the people to unite
under one king, Kenneth MacAlpin. The term Scotland began to be used to
describe that country. 🙶

1) After the Romans left in AD 410, Britain was
   invaded by tribes from northern Europe
   — the Jutes, Angles and Saxons.

2) By about AD 600, Anglo-Saxon kingdoms
   were established in England.

3) At this time, Irish missionaries,
   such as St Patrick and
   St Columba, preached
   about Christianity in Britain.

4) The Vikings began raiding
   Britain in AD 789.

5) Alfred the Great united the Anglo-
   Saxons and defeated the Vikings.

Northern European
invasions of Britain

The Norman Conquest

❝ In 1066, an invasion led by William, the Duke of Normandy (in what is now northern France), defeated Harold, the Saxon king of England, at the Battle of Hastings. Harold was killed in the battle. William became king of England and is known as William the Conqueror. The battle is commemorated in a great piece of embroidery, known as the Bayeux Tapestry, which can still be seen in France today.

The Norman Conquest was the last successful foreign invasion of England and led to many changes in government and social structures in England. Norman French, the language of the new ruling class, influenced the development of the English language as we know it today. Initially the Normans also conquered Wales, but the Welsh gradually won territory back. The Scots and the Normans fought on the border between England and Scotland; the Normans took over some land on the border but did not invade Scotland.

William sent people all over England to draw up lists of all the towns and villages. The people who lived there, who owned the land and what animals they owned were also listed. This was called the Domesday Book. It still exists today and gives a picture of society in England just after the Norman Conquest. ❞

1) The Norman Conquest of England took place in 1066.

2) The Saxon king, Harold, was killed in the Battle of Hastings, and William the Conqueror became king of England.

3) The Battle of Hastings is commemorated in the Bayeux Tapestry (right).

The Bayeux Tapestry is made of linen cloth embroidered with coloured wool, and is nearly 70 metres (230 feet) long

The Middle Ages

War at home and abroad

❝ The period after the Norman Conquest up until about 1485 is called the Middle Ages (or the medieval period). It was a time of almost constant war.

The English kings fought with the Welsh, Scottish and Irish noblemen for control of their lands. In Wales, the English were able to establish their rule. In 1284 King Edward I of England introduced the Statute of Rhuddlan, which annexed Wales to the Crown of England. Huge castles, including Conwy and Caernarvon, were built to maintain this power. By the middle of the 15th century the last Welsh rebellions had been defeated. English laws and the English language were introduced.

In Scotland, the English kings were less successful. In 1314 the Scottish, led by Robert the Bruce, defeated the English at the Battle of Bannockburn, and Scotland remained unconquered by the English.

At the beginning of the Middle Ages, Ireland was an independent country. The English first went to Ireland as troops to help the Irish king and remained to build their own settlements. By 1200, the English ruled an area of Ireland known as the Pale, around Dublin. Some of the important lords in other parts of Ireland accepted the authority of the English king.

During the Middle Ages, the English kings also fought a number of wars abroad. Many knights took part in the Crusades, in which European Christians fought for control of the Holy Land. English kings also fought a long war with France, called the Hundred Years War (even though it actually lasted 116 years). One of the most famous battles of the Hundred Years War was the Battle of Agincourt in 1415, where King Henry V's vastly outnumbered English army defeated the French. The English left France in the 1450s.

1) King Edward I of England annexed Wales in 1284.

2) The Scottish defeated the English at the Battle of Bannockburn in 1314, and Scotland remained unconquered.

3) By 1200, the English ruled an area of Ireland called the Pale.

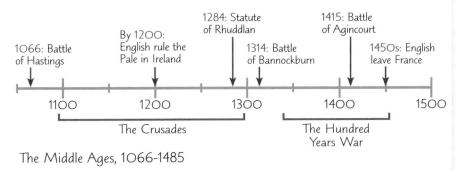

1066: Battle of Hastings

By 1200: English rule the Pale in Ireland

1284: Statute of Rhuddlan

1314: Battle of Bannockburn

1415: Battle of Agincourt

1450s: English leave France

1100   1200   1300   1400   1500

The Crusades

The Hundred Years War

The Middle Ages, 1066-1485

The Black Death

❝ The Normans used a system of land ownership known as feudalism. The king gave land to his lords in return for help in war. Landowners had to send certain numbers of men to serve in the army. Some peasants had their own land but most were serfs. They had a small area of their lord's land where they could grow food. In return, they had to work for their lord and could not move away. The same system developed in southern Scotland. In the north of Scotland and Ireland, land was owned by members of the 'clans' (prominent families).

In 1348, a disease, probably a form of plague, came to Britain. This was known as the Black Death. One third of the population of England died and a similar proportion in Scotland and Wales. This was one of the worst disasters ever to strike Britain. Following the Black Death, the smaller population meant there was less need to grow cereal crops. There were labour shortages and peasants began to demand higher wages. New social classes appeared, including owners of large areas of land (later called the gentry), and people left the countryside to live in the towns. In the towns, growing wealth led to the development of a strong middle class.

In Ireland, the Black Death killed many in the Pale and, for a time, the area controlled by the English became smaller. ❞

1) Feudalism was a system of land ownership in which the king gave his lords land, and in return they helped him during wars.

2) The Black Death came to Britain in 1348.

3) In England, a third of the population died. Similar proportions died in Scotland and Wales too, and also many in the Pale.

4) After the Black Death there were fewer labourers to work, so peasants demanded higher wages.

5) New social classes appeared, including the gentry (who owned large areas of land).

Legal and political changes

❝ In the Middle Ages, Parliament began to develop into the institution it is today. Its origins can be traced to the king's council of advisers, which included important noblemen and the leaders of the Church.

There were few formal limits to the king's power until 1215. In that year, King John was forced by his noblemen to agree to a number of demands. The result was a charter of rights called the Magna Carta (which means the Great Charter). The Magna Carta established the idea that even the king was subject to the law. It protected the rights of the nobility and restricted the king's power to collect taxes or to make or change laws. In future, the king would need to involve his noblemen in decisions.

In England, parliaments were called for the king to consult his nobles, particularly when the king needed to raise money. The numbers attending Parliament increased and two separate parts, known as Houses, were established. The nobility, great landowners and bishops sat in the House of Lords. Knights, who were usually smaller landowners, and wealthy people from towns and cities were elected to sit in the House of Commons. Only a small part of the population was able to join in electing the members of the Commons.

A similar Parliament developed in Scotland. It had three Houses, called Estates: the lords, the commons and the clergy.

This was also a time of development in the legal system. The principle that judges are independent of the government began to be established. In England, judges developed 'common law' by a process of precedence (that is, following previous decisions) and tradition. In Scotland, the legal system developed slightly differently and laws were 'codified' (that is, written down).

1) Modern Parliament has its origins in the king's council of advisers.

2) In 1215, King John was forced to agree to the Magna Carta.

3) The Magna Carta restricted the king's power and stated that even the king had to obey the law.

4) In England, Parliament split into two Houses, the Commons and the Lords.

5) Only a small part of the population could elect members of the Commons.

King John signed the Magna Carta in 1215

A distinct identity

66 The Middle Ages saw the development of a national culture and identity. After the Norman Conquest, the king and his noblemen had spoken Norman French and the peasants had continued to speak Anglo-Saxon.   Gradually these two languages combined to become one English language.   Some words in modern English — for example, 'park' and 'beauty' — are based on Norman French words.   Others — for example, 'apple', 'cow' and 'summer' — are based on Anglo-Saxon words.   In modern English there are often two words with very similar meanings, one from French and one from Anglo-Saxon.   'Demand' (French) and 'ask' (Anglo-Saxon) are examples.   By 1400, in England, official documents were being written in English, and English had become the preferred language of the royal court and Parliament.

In the years leading up to 1400, Geoffrey Chaucer wrote a series of poems in English about a group of people going to Canterbury on a pilgrimage. The people decided to tell each other stories on the journey, and the poems describe the travellers and some of the stories they told.   This collection of poems is called *The Canterbury Tales*.   It was one of the first books to be printed by William Caxton, the first person in England to print books using a printing press.   Many of the stories are still popular.   Some have been made into plays and television programmes.

In Scotland, many people continued to speak Gaelic and the Scots language also developed.   A number of poets began to write in the Scots language. One example is John Barbour, who wrote *The Bruce* about the Battle of Bannockburn.

The Middle Ages also saw a change in the type of buildings in Britain.   Castles were built in many places in Britain and Ireland, partly for defence.   Today many are in ruins, although some, such as Windsor and Edinburgh, are still in use.   Great cathedrals — for example, Lincoln Cathedral — were also built, and many of these are still used for worship.   Several of the cathedrals had windows of stained glass, telling stories about the Bible and Christian saints. The glass in York Minster is a famous example.

During this period, England was an important trading nation.   English wool became a very important export.   People came to England from abroad to trade and also to work.   Many had special skills, such as weavers from France, engineers from Germany, glass manufacturers from Italy and canal builders from Holland. 99

1) English is a combination of Anglo-Saxon and Norman French. By 1400, official documents in England were written in English.

2) *The Canterbury Tales*, by Geoffrey Chaucer, is a series of English poems written just before 1400.

Edinburgh Castle is still in use today

3) *The Bruce* is a poem about the Battle of Bannockburn by the Scottish poet John Barbour. It is written in the Scots language.

4) Castles and cathedrals were built in the Middle Ages and some are still in use today. Examples of these are Windsor Castle, Edinburgh Castle and Lincoln Cathedral.

The Wars of the Roses

“ In 1455, a civil war was begun to decide who should be king of England. It was fought between the supporters of two families: the House of Lancaster and the House of York. This war was called the Wars of the Roses, because the symbol of Lancaster was a red rose and the symbol of York was a white rose. The war ended with the Battle of Bosworth Field in 1485. King Richard III of the House of York was killed in the battle and Henry Tudor, the leader of the House of Lancaster, became King Henry VII. Henry then married King Richard's niece, Elizabeth of York, and united the two families. Henry was the first king of the House of Tudor. The symbol of the House of Tudor was a red rose with a white rose inside it as a sign that the Houses of York and Lancaster were now allies. ”

1) The Wars of the Roses were fought between 1455 and 1485.

2) Henry Tudor won the Battle of Bosworth Field in 1485, defeating King Richard III, and became King Henry VII.

The rose of the House of Tudor

The Tudors and Stuarts

Religious conflicts

❝ After his victory in the Wars of the Roses, Henry VII wanted to make sure that England remained peaceful and that his position as king was secure. He deliberately strengthened the central administration of England and reduced the power of the nobles. He was thrifty and built up the monarchy's financial reserves. When he died, his son Henry VIII continued the policy of centralising power.

Henry VIII was most famous for breaking away from the Church of Rome and marrying six times.

The six wives of Henry VIII

Catherine of Aragon — Catherine was a Spanish princess. She and Henry had a number of children but only one, Mary, survived. When Catherine was too old to give him another child, Henry decided to divorce her, hoping that another wife would give him a son to be his heir.

Anne Boleyn — Anne Boleyn was English. She and Henry had one daughter, Elizabeth. Anne was unpopular in the country and was accused of taking lovers. She was executed at the Tower of London.

Tip: Make sure you learn about Henry VIII's wives and his children.

Jane Seymour — Henry married Jane after Anne's execution. She gave Henry the son he wanted, Edward, but she died shortly after the birth.

Anne of Cleves — Anne was a German princess. Henry married her for political reasons but divorced her soon after.

Catherine Howard — Catherine was a cousin of Anne Boleyn. She was also accused of taking lovers and executed.

Catherine Parr — Catherine was a widow who married Henry late in his life. She survived him and married again but died soon after.

To divorce his first wife, Henry needed the approval of the Pope. When the Pope refused, Henry established the Church of England. In this new Church, the king, not the Pope, would have the power to appoint bishops and order how people should worship.

At the same time the Reformation was happening across Europe. This was a movement against the authority of the Pope and the ideas and practices of the Roman Catholic Church. The Protestants formed their own churches. They read the Bible in their own languages instead of in Latin; they did not pray to saints or at shrines; and they believed that a person's own relationship with God was more important than submitting to the authority of the Church. Protestant ideas gradually gained strength in England, Wales and Scotland during the 16th century.

In Ireland, however, attempts by the English to impose Protestantism (alongside efforts to introduce the English system of laws about the inheritance of land) led to rebellion from the Irish chieftains, and much brutal fighting followed.

During the reign of Henry VIII, Wales became formally united with England by the Act for the Government of Wales. The Welsh sent representatives to the House of Commons and the Welsh legal system was reformed.

Henry VIII was succeeded by his son Edward VI, who was strongly Protestant. During his reign, the Book of Common Prayer was written to be used in the Church of England. A version of this book is still used in some churches today. Edward died at the age of 15 after ruling for just over six years, and his half-sister Mary became queen. Mary was a devout Catholic and persecuted Protestants (for this reason, she became known as 'Bloody Mary'). Mary also died after a short reign and the next monarch was her half-sister, Elizabeth, the daughter of Henry VIII and Anne Boleyn.

1) Henry VIII was king from 21 April 1509 to 28 January 1547.

2) Henry VIII established the Church of England, which had the monarch as its head.

3) Protestantism spread through Europe during the Reformation. Protestant ideas grew popular in England, Wales and Scotland in the 16th century.

4) During Henry VIII's reign, Wales became formally united with England by the Act for the Government of Wales.

5) Three of Henry VIII's children reigned after him: Edward VI, Mary I and Elizabeth I.

Mary I was also known as 'Bloody Mary'

Queen Elizabeth I

❝ Queen Elizabeth I was a Protestant. She re-established the Church of England as the official Church in England. Everyone had to attend their local church and there were laws about the type of religious services and the prayers which could be said, but Elizabeth did not ask about people's real beliefs. She succeeded in finding a balance between the views of Catholics and the more extreme Protestants. In this way, she avoided any serious religious conflict within England. Elizabeth became one of the most popular monarchs in English history, particularly after 1588, when the English defeated the Spanish Armada (a large fleet of ships), which had been sent by Spain to conquer England and restore Catholicism.

The Reformation in Scotland and Mary, Queen of Scots

Scotland had also been strongly influenced by Protestant ideas. In 1560, the predominantly Protestant Scottish Parliament abolished the authority of the Pope in Scotland and Roman Catholic religious services became illegal. A Protestant Church of Scotland with an elected leadership was established but, unlike in England, this was not a state Church.

The queen of Scotland, Mary Stuart (often now called 'Mary, Queen of Scots') was a Catholic. She was only a week old when her father died and she became queen. Much of her childhood was spent in France. When she returned to Scotland, she was the centre of a power struggle between different groups. When her husband was murdered, Mary was suspected of involvement and fled to England. She gave her throne to her Protestant son, James VI of Scotland. Mary was Elizabeth I's cousin and hoped that Elizabeth might help her, but Elizabeth suspected Mary of wanting to take over the English throne, and kept her a prisoner for 20 years. Mary was eventually executed, accused of plotting against Elizabeth I. ❞

1) Elizabeth I found a balance between Catholic and Protestant views, and so she avoided serious religious conflict in England.

2) The English defeated the Spanish Armada in 1588.

3) The Protestant Church of Scotland was established in 1560.

4) Mary, Queen of Scots, was Elizabeth I's cousin and the mother of James VI of Scotland.

5) Mary was accused of plotting against Elizabeth and executed.

Exploration, poetry and drama

❝ The Elizabethan period in England was a time of growing patriotism: a feeling of pride in being English. English explorers sought new trade routes and tried to expand British trade into the Spanish colonies in the Americas. Sir Francis Drake, one of the commanders in the defeat of the Spanish Armada, was one of the founders of England's naval tradition. His ship, the *Golden Hind*, was one of the first to sail right around ('circumnavigate') the world. In Elizabeth I's time, English settlers first began to colonise the eastern coast of America. This colonisation, particularly by people who disagreed with the religious views of the next two kings, greatly increased in the next century.

The Elizabethan period is also remembered for the richness of its poetry and drama, especially the plays and poems of William Shakespeare.

William Shakespeare (1564-1616)

Shakespeare was born in Stratford-upon-Avon, England. He was a playwright and actor and wrote many poems and plays. His most famous plays include *A Midsummer Night's Dream*, *Hamlet*, *Macbeth* and *Romeo and Juliet*. He also dramatised significant events from the past, but he did not focus solely on kings and queens. He was one of the first to portray ordinary Englishmen and women. Shakespeare had a great influence on the English language and invented many words that are still common today. Lines from his plays and poems which are often still quoted include:

- Once more unto the breach (*Henry V*)
- To be or not to be (*Hamlet*)
- A rose by any other name (*Romeo and Juliet*)
- All the world's a stage (*As You Like It*)
- The darling buds of May (*Sonnet 18 - Shall I Compare Thee To A Summer's Day*).

Many people regard Shakespeare as the greatest playwright of all time. His plays and poems are still performed and studied in Britain and other countries today. The Globe Theatre in London is a modern copy of the theatres in which his plays were first performed.

❞

1) Exploration was popular during Elizabeth I's reign. Sir Francis Drake sailed right around the world in the *Golden Hind*.

2) English colonists began to settle on the east coast of America.

3) William Shakespeare was a famous playwright and poet. He was one of the first writers to write to about ordinary English people.

James VI and I

66 Elizabeth I never married and so had no children of her own to inherit her throne. When she died in 1603 her heir was her cousin James VI of Scotland. He became King James I of England, Wales and Ireland but Scotland remained a separate country.

The King James Bible

One achievement of King James' reign was a new translation of the Bible into English. This translation is known as the 'King James Version' or the 'Authorised Version'. It was not the first English Bible but is a version which continues to be used in many Protestant churches today.

Ireland

During this period, Ireland was an almost completely Catholic country. Henry VII and Henry VIII had extended English control outside the Pale (see page 17) and had established English authority over the whole country. Henry VIII took the title 'King of Ireland'. English laws were introduced and local leaders were expected to follow the instructions of the Lord Lieutenants in Dublin.

During the reigns of Elizabeth I and James I, many people in Ireland opposed rule by the Protestant government in England. There were a number of rebellions. The English government encouraged Scottish and English Protestants to settle in Ulster, the northern province of Ireland, taking over the land from Catholic landholders. These settlements were known as plantations. Many of the new settlers came from south-west Scotland and other land was given to companies based in London. James later organised similar plantations in several other parts of Ireland. This had serious long-term consequences for the history of England, Scotland and Ireland. 99

1) During the reign of James I, a new translation of the Bible into English was produced — the 'King James Version'.

2) Ireland was almost completely Catholic during James I's reign.

3) English and Scottish Protestants were encouraged to move to Ulster. They lived in settlements called plantations.

The rise of Parliament

❝ Elizabeth I was very skilled at managing Parliament. During her reign, she was successful in balancing her wishes and views against those of the House of Lords and those of the House of Commons, which was increasingly Protestant in its views.

James I and his son Charles I were less skilled politically. Both believed in the 'Divine Right of Kings': the idea that the king was directly appointed by God to rule. They thought that the king should be able to act without having to seek approval from Parliament. When Charles I inherited the thrones of England, Wales, Ireland and Scotland, he tried to rule in line with this principle. When he could not get Parliament to agree with his religious and foreign policies, he tried to rule without Parliament at all. For 11 years, he found ways in which to raise money without Parliament's approval but eventually trouble in Scotland meant that he had to recall Parliament.

The beginning of the English Civil War

Charles I wanted the worship of the Church of England to include more ceremony and introduced a revised Prayer Book. He tried to impose this Prayer Book on the Presbyterian Church in Scotland and this led to serious unrest. A Scottish army was formed and Charles could not find the money he needed for his own army without the help of Parliament. In 1640, he recalled Parliament to ask it for funds. Many in Parliament were Puritans, a group of Protestants who advocated strict and simple religious doctrine and worship. They did not agree with the king's religious views and disliked his reforms of the Church of England. Parliament refused to give the king the money he asked for, even after the Scottish army invaded England.

Another rebellion began in Ireland because the Roman Catholics in Ireland were afraid of the growing power of the Puritans. Parliament took this opportunity to demand control of the English army — a change that would have transferred substantial power from the king to Parliament. In response, Charles I entered the House of Commons and tried to arrest five parliamentary leaders, but they had been warned and were not there. (No monarch has set foot in the Commons since.) Civil war between the king and Parliament could not now be avoided and began in 1642. The country split into those who supported the king (the Cavaliers) and those who supported Parliament (the Roundheads). 99

1) Charles I believed in the 'Divine Right of Kings' — he thought that the king was appointed by God and that he could act without the approval of Parliament.

2) Charles introduced a revised Prayer Book and tried to impose it on the Scottish Presbyterian Church, but this led to unrest.

3) Following a rebellion in Ireland, Parliament demanded control of the English army, but Charles refused.

4) Civil war broke out in 1642. The king's supporters were called the Cavaliers and Parliament's were called the Roundheads.

Oliver Cromwell and the English Republic

66 The king's army was defeated at the Battles of Marston Moor and Naseby. By 1646, it was clear that Parliament had won the war. Charles was held prisoner by the parliamentary army. He was still unwilling to reach any agreement with Parliament and in 1649 he was executed.

England declared itself a republic, called the Commonwealth. It no longer had a monarch. For a time, it was not totally clear how the country would be governed. For now, the army was in control. One of its generals, Oliver Cromwell, was sent to Ireland, where the revolt which had begun in 1641 still continued and where there was still a Royalist army. Cromwell was successful in establishing the authority of the English Parliament but did this with such violence that even today Cromwell remains a controversial figure in Ireland.

The Scots had not agreed to the execution of Charles I and declared his son Charles II to be king. He was crowned king of Scotland and led a Scottish army into England. Cromwell defeated this army in the Battles of Dunbar and Worcester. Charles II escaped from Worcester, famously hiding in an oak tree on one occasion, and eventually fled to Europe. Parliament now controlled Scotland as well as England and Wales.

After his campaign in Ireland and victory over Charles II at Worcester, Cromwell was recognised as the leader of the new republic. He was given the title of Lord Protector and ruled until his death in 1658. When Cromwell died, his son, Richard, became Lord Protector in his place but was not able to control the army or the government. Although Britain had been a republic for 11 years, without Oliver Cromwell there was no clear leader or system of government. Many people in the country wanted stability. People began to talk about the need for a king. 🙶🙶

1) Parliament defeated Charles I's army at the Battles of Marston Moor and Naseby. Parliament had won the civil war by 1646.

2) Charles I was executed in 1649. England had no monarch and became a republic, called the Commonwealth.

3) Charles's son, Charles II, invaded England, but was defeated by Oliver Cromwell at the Battles of Dunbar and Worcester.

4) Oliver Cromwell ruled the Commonwealth until his death in 1658.

5) Cromwell's son, Richard, succeeded him as Lord Protector, but he couldn't control the army or the government.

Oliver Cromwell is still a controversial figure in Ireland because he violently crushed a revolt there

The Restoration

🙶🙶 In May 1660, Parliament invited Charles II to come back from exile in the Netherlands. He was crowned King Charles II of England, Wales, Scotland and Ireland. Charles II made it clear that he had 'no wish to go on his travels again'. He understood that he could not always do as he wished but would sometimes need to reach agreement with Parliament. Generally, Parliament supported his policies. The Church of England again became the established official Church. Both Roman Catholics and Puritans were kept out of power.

During Charles II's reign, in 1665, there was a major outbreak of plague in London. Thousands of people died, especially in poorer areas. The following year, a great fire destroyed much of the city, including many churches and St Paul's Cathedral. London was rebuilt with a new St Paul's, which was designed by a famous architect, Sir Christopher Wren. Samuel Pepys wrote about these events in a diary which was later published and is still read today.

The Habeas Corpus Act became law in 1679. This was a very important piece of legislation which remains relevant today. Habeas corpus is Latin for 'you must present the person in court'. The Act guaranteed that no one could be held prisoner unlawfully. Every prisoner has a right to a court hearing.

Charles II was interested in science. During his reign, the Royal Society was formed to promote 'natural knowledge'. This is the oldest surviving scientific society in the world. Among its early members were Sir Edmund Halley, who successfully predicted the return of the comet now called Halley's Comet, and Sir Isaac Newton.

Isaac Newton (1643-1727)

Born in Lincolnshire, eastern England, Isaac Newton first became interested in science when he studied at Cambridge University. He became an important figure in the field. His most famous published work was *Philosophiae Naturalis Principia Mathematica* ('Mathematical Principles of Natural Philosophy'), which showed how gravity applied to the whole universe. Newton also discovered that white light is made up of the colours of the rainbow. Many of his discoveries are still important for modern science.

A statue of Isaac Newton at Cambridge University, where he studied

©iStockphoto.com/Anthony Baggett

1) In 1660, Parliament invited Charles II back from exile.

2) In 1665, there was an outbreak of plague in London.

3) In 1666, a great fire destroyed a lot of London, including St Paul's Cathedral. When London was rebuilt, a new St Paul's was designed by Sir Christopher Wren.

4) In 1679, the Habeas Corpus Act became law. The Act means that every prisoner has a right to a court hearing.

5) The Royal Society, which is the world's oldest surviving scientific society, was founded during Charles II's reign.

6) Isaac Newton, an early member of the Royal Society, showed how gravity applied to the whole universe.

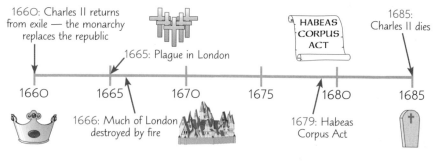

Events during the reign of Charles II, 1660-1685

A Catholic king

❝ Charles II had no legitimate children. He died in 1685 and his brother, James, who was a Roman Catholic, became King James II in England, Wales and Ireland and King James VII of Scotland. James favoured Roman Catholics and allowed them to be army officers, which an Act of Parliament had forbidden. He did not seek to reach agreements with Parliament and arrested some of the bishops of the Church of England. People in England worried that James wanted to make England a Catholic country once more. However, his heirs were his two daughters, who were both firmly Protestant, and people thought that this meant there would soon be a Protestant monarch again. Then, James's wife had a son. Suddenly, it seemed likely that the next monarch would not be a Protestant after all.

The Glorious Revolution

James II's elder daughter, Mary, was married to her cousin William of Orange, the Protestant ruler of the Netherlands. In 1688, important Protestants in England asked William to invade England and proclaim himself king. When William reached England, there was no resistance. James fled to France and William took over the throne, becoming William III in England, Wales and Ireland, and William II of Scotland. William ruled jointly with Mary. This event was later called the 'Glorious Revolution' because there was no fighting in England and because it guaranteed the power of Parliament, ending the threat of a monarch ruling on his or her own as he or she wished. James II wanted to regain the throne and invaded Ireland with the help of a French army. William defeated James II at the Battle of the Boyne in Ireland in 1690, an event which is still celebrated by some in Northern Ireland today. William re-conquered Ireland and James fled back to France. Many restrictions were placed on the Roman Catholic Church in Ireland and Irish Catholics were unable to take part in the government.

There was also support for James in Scotland. An attempt at an armed rebellion in support of James was quickly defeated at Killiecrankie. All Scottish clans were required formally to accept William as king by taking an oath. The MacDonalds of Glencoe were late in taking the oath and were all killed. The memory of this massacre meant some Scots distrusted the new government.

Some continued to believe that James was the rightful king, particularly in Scotland. Some joined him in exile in France; others were secret supporters. James' supporters became known as Jacobites. 99

1) Charles II died in 1685 and his brother became King James II.
2) James II was a Catholic. People in England were worried that James would make England a Catholic country again.
3) In 1688, William of Orange (the Protestant ruler of the Netherlands) was asked to invade England and become king.
4) James II fled, but tried to regain the throne by invading Ireland.
5) William of Orange (now William III of England) defeated James II at the Battle of the Boyne in 1690.
6) James II's supporters in Scotland were defeated at Killiecrankie.
7) Supporters of James II became known as Jacobites.

A global power

Constitutional monarchy — the Bill of Rights

❝ At the coronation of William and Mary, a Declaration of Rights was read. This confirmed that the king would no longer be able to raise taxes or administer justice without agreement from Parliament. The balance of power between monarch and Parliament had now permanently changed. The Bill of Rights, 1689, confirmed the rights of Parliament and the limits of the king's power. Parliament took control of who could be monarch and declared that the king or queen must be a Protestant. A new Parliament had to be elected at least every three years (later this became seven years and now it is five years). Every year the monarch had to ask Parliament to renew funding for the army and the navy.

These changes meant that, to be able to govern effectively, the monarch needed to have advisers, or ministers, who would be able to ensure a majority of votes in the House of Commons and the House of Lords. There were two main groups in Parliament, known as the Whigs and the Tories. (The modern Conservative Party is still sometimes referred to as the Tories.) This was the beginning of party politics.

This was also an important time for the development of a free press (newspapers and other publications which are not controlled by the government). From 1695, newspapers were allowed to operate without a government licence. Increasing numbers of newspapers began to be published.

The laws passed after the Glorious Revolution are the beginning of what is called 'constitutional monarchy'. The monarch remained very important but was no longer able to insist on particular policies or actions if Parliament did not agree. After William III, the ministers gradually became more important than the monarch but this was not a democracy in the modern sense. The number of people who had the right to vote for members of Parliament was still very small. Only men who owned property of a certain value were able to vote. No women at all had the vote. Some constituencies were controlled by a single wealthy family. These were called 'pocket boroughs'. Other constituencies had hardly any voters and were called 'rotten boroughs'.

A growing population

This was a time when many people left Britain and Ireland to settle in new colonies in America and elsewhere, but others came to live in Britain. The first Jews to come to Britain since the Middle Ages settled in London in 16ᶠ

Between 1680 and 1720 many refugees called Huguenots came from France. They were Protestants and had been persecuted for their religion. Many were educated and skilled and worked as scientists, in banking, or in weaving or other crafts. 99

1) The Bill of Rights, 1689, stated the rights of Parliament and the limits of the king's power.

2) Parliament controlled who could be monarch, and every year the monarch had to ask Parliament to renew funding for the army and the navy.

3) In Parliament, two main groups formed — the Whigs and the Tories.

4) Most people could not vote at this time. Some constituencies were controlled by a single wealthy family ('pocket boroughs'), and others had hardly any voters ('rotten boroughs').

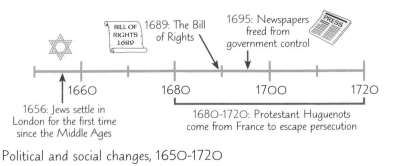

Political and social changes, 1650-1720

The Act or Treaty of Union in Scotland

66 William and Mary's successor, Queen Anne, had no surviving children. This created uncertainty over the succession in England, Wales and Ireland and in Scotland. The Act of Union, known as the Treaty of Union in Scotland, was therefore agreed in 1707, creating the Kingdom of Great Britain. Although Scotland was no longer an independent country, it kept its own legal and education systems and Presbyterian Church.

The Prime Minister

When Queen Anne died in 1714, Parliament chose a German, George I, to be the next king, because he was Anne's nearest Protestant relative. An attempt by Scottish Jacobites to put James II's son on the throne instead was quickly defeated. George I did not speak very good English and this increased his need to rely on his ministers. The most important minister in Parliament became known as the Prime Minister. The first man to be called this was Sir Robert Walpole, who was Prime Minister from 1721 to 1742.

The rebellion of the clans

In 1745 there was another attempt to put a Stuart king back on the throne in place of George I's son, George II. Charles Edward Stuart (Bonnie Prince Charlie), the grandson of James II, landed in Scotland. He was supported by clansmen from the Scottish highlands and raised an army. Charles initially had some successes but was defeated by George II's army at the Battle of Culloden in 1746. Charles escaped back to Europe.

The clans lost a lot of their power and influence after Culloden. Chieftains became landlords if they had the favour of the English king, and clansmen became tenants who had to pay for the land they used.

A process began which became known as the 'Highland Clearances'. Many Scottish landlords destroyed individual small farms (known as 'crofts') to make space for large flocks of sheep and cattle. Evictions became very common in the early 19th century. Many Scottish people left for North America at this time.

1) In 1707, the Act of Union united Scotland with England and Wales to create the Kingdom of Great Britain.

2) Parliament's first Prime Minister was Sir Robert Walpole, who held the position from 1721 to 1742.

3) In 1745, Charles Edward Stuart (James II's grandson) tried to take the throne with the help of Scottish clansmen.

4) He was defeated by George II's army at the Battle of Culloden in 1746.

5) During the 'Highland Clearances', many Scottish landlords evicted people from their individual small farms and used the land to farm large flocks of animals.

Charles Edward Stuart was also known as Bonnie Prince Charlie

“

Robert Burns (1759-96)

Known in Scotland as 'The Bard', Robert Burns was a Scottish poet. He wrote in the Scots language, English with some Scottish words, and standard English. He also revised a lot of traditional folk songs by changing or adding lyrics. Burns' best-known work is probably the song *Auld Lang Syne*, which is sung by people in the UK and other countries when they are celebrating the New Year (or Hogmanay as it is called in Scotland).

The Enlightenment

During the 18th century, new ideas about politics, philosophy and science were developed. This is often called 'the Enlightenment'. Many of the great thinkers of the Enlightenment were Scottish. Adam Smith developed ideas about economics which are still referred to today. David Hume's ideas about human nature continue to influence philosophers. Scientific discoveries, such as James Watt's work on steam power, helped the progress of the Industrial Revolution. One of the most important principles of the Enlightenment was that everyone should have the right to their own political and religious beliefs and that the state should not try to dictate to them. This continues to be an important principle in the UK today. ”

1) In the 18th century, new ideas developed about politics, philosophy and science. This is called 'the Enlightenment'.

2) Scientific discoveries in this period helped the progress of the Industrial Revolution (see pages 37-38).

3) An important principle of the Enlightenment was the idea that everyone should have the right to their own political and religious beliefs.

Robert Burns was a Scottish poet who wrote the song 'Auld Lang Syne'

The Industrial Revolution

" Before the 18th century, agriculture was the biggest source of employment in Britain. There were many cottage industries, where people worked from home to produce goods such as cloth and lace.

The Industrial Revolution was the rapid development of industry in Britain in the 18th and 19th centuries. Britain was the first country to industrialise on a large scale. It happened because of the development of machinery and the use of steam power. Agriculture and the manufacturing of goods became mechanised. This made things more efficient and increased production. Coal and other raw materials were needed to power the new factories. Many people moved from the countryside and started working in the mining and manufacturing industries.

The development of the Bessemer process for the mass production of steel led to the development of the shipbuilding industry and the railways. Manufacturing jobs became the main source of employment in Britain.

Richard Arkwright (1732-92)

Born in 1732, Arkwright originally trained and worked as a barber. He was able to dye hair and make wigs. When wigs became less popular, he started to work in textiles. He improved the original carding machine. Carding is the process of preparing fibres for spinning into yarn and fabric. He also developed horse-driven spinning mills that used only one machine. This increased the efficiency of production. Later, he used the steam engine to power machinery. Arkwright is particularly remembered for the efficient and profitable way that he ran his factories.

Better transport links were needed to transport raw materials and manufactured goods. Canals were built to link the factories to towns and cities and to the ports, particularly in the new industrial areas in the middle and north of England.

Working conditions during the Industrial Revolution were very poor. There were no laws to protect employees, who were often forced to work long hours in dangerous situations. Children also worked and were treated in the same way as adults. Sometimes they were treated even more harshly.

This was also a time of increased colonisation overseas. Captain James Cook mapped the coast of Australia and a few colonies were established there.

Britain gained control over Canada, and the East India Company, originally set up to trade, gained control of large parts of India. Colonies began to be established in southern Africa.

Britain traded all over the world and began to import more goods. Sugar and tobacco came from North America and the West Indies; textiles, tea and spices came from India and the area that is today called Indonesia. Trading and settlements overseas sometimes brought Britain into conflict with other countries, particularly France, which was expanding and trading in a similar way in many of the same areas of the world.

Sake Dean Mahomet (1759-1851)

Mahomet was born in 1759 and grew up in the Bengal region of India. He served in the Bengal army and came to Britain in 1782. He then moved to Ireland and eloped with an Irish girl called Jane Daly in 1786, returning to England at the turn of the century. In 1810 he opened the Hindoostane Coffee House in George Street, London. It was the first curry house to open in Britain. Mahomet and his wife also introduced 'shampooing', the Indian art of head massage, to Britain.

1) During the Industrial Revolution, agriculture and manufacturing became mechanised (a lot of the work was done by machines rather than by people).

2) The Bessemer process (for mass producing steel) helped the development of the shipbuilding industry and the railways.

3) Richard Arkwright improved the original machine for carding (the process of preparing fibres for spinning into yarn).

4) Canals were built so that raw materials and goods could be transported between factories, towns, cities and ports.

5) During this time, James Cook mapped the coast of Australia, and Britain gained control of Canada. The East India Company took control of large parts of India.

6) Britain imported sugar and tobacco from North America and the West Indies. Textiles, tea and spices were imported from India and the area that is now called Indonesia.

7) Sake Dean Mahomet opened Britain's first curry house in 1810.

The slave trade

" This commercial expansion and prosperity was sustained in part by the booming slave trade. While slavery was illegal within Britain itself, by the 18th century it was a fully established overseas industry, dominated by Britain and the American colonies.

Slaves came primarily from West Africa. Travelling on British ships in horrible conditions, they were taken to America and the Caribbean, where they were made to work on tobacco and sugar plantations. The living and working conditions for slaves were very bad. Many slaves tried to escape and others revolted against their owners in protest at their terrible treatment.

There were, however, people in Britain who opposed the slave trade. The first formal anti-slavery groups were set up by the Quakers in the late 1700s, and they petitioned Parliament to ban the practice. William Wilberforce, an evangelical Christian and a member of Parliament, also played an important part in changing the law. Along with other abolitionists (people who supported the abolition of slavery), he succeeded in turning public opinion against the slave trade. In 1807, it became illegal to trade slaves in British ships or from British ports, and in 1833 the Emancipation Act abolished slavery throughout the British Empire. The Royal Navy stopped slave ships from other countries, freed the slaves and punished the slave traders. After 1833, 2 million Indian and Chinese workers were employed to replace the freed slaves. They worked on sugar plantations in the Caribbean, in mines in South Africa, on railways in East Africa and in the army in Kenya. "

1) Britain and the American colonies dominated the overseas slave trade in the 18th century, but slavery was illegal within Britain itself.

2) Slaves were taken from West Africa to plantations in America and the Caribbean. The slaves worked in terrible conditions.

3) People who opposed slavery were called abolitionists.

4) William Wilberforce (who was a member of Parliament) turned public opinion against the slave trade.

5) It became illegal to trade slaves in British ships or from British ports in 1807.

6) The Emancipation Act (1833) abolished slavery in the British Empire.

7) Around 2 million Indian and Chinese workers were employed to replace the slaves.

The American War of Independence

66 By the 1760s, there were substantial British colonies in North America. The colonies were wealthy and largely in control of their own affairs. Many of the colonist families had originally gone to North America in order to have religious freedom. They were well educated and interested in ideas of liberty. The British government wanted to tax the colonies. The colonists saw this as an attack on their freedom and said there should be 'no taxation without representation' in the British Parliament. Parliament tried to compromise by repealing some of the taxes, but relationships between the British government and the colonies continued to worsen. Fighting broke out between the colonists and the British forces. In 1776, 13 American colonies declared their independence, stating that people had a right to establish their own governments. The colonists eventually defeated the British army and Britain recognised the colonies' independence in 1783.

War with France

During the 18th century, Britain fought a number of wars with France. In 1789, there was a revolution in France and the new French government soon declared war on Britain. Napoleon, who became Emperor of France, continued the war. Britain's navy fought against combined French and Spanish fleets, winning the Battle of Trafalgar in 1805. Admiral Nelson was in charge of the British fleet at Trafalgar and was killed in the battle. Nelson's Column in Trafalgar Square, London, is a monument to him. His ship, *HMS Victory*, can be visited in Portsmouth. The British army also fought against the French. In 1815, the French Wars ended with the defeat of the Emperor Napoleon by the Duke of Wellington at the Battle of Waterloo. Wellington was known as the Iron Duke and later became Prime Minister. 99

1) In 1776, 13 American colonies declared their independence from Britain.

2) By 1783 the American colonies had defeated the British army, and Britain recognised the colonies' independence.

3) On 21 October 1805, the British navy defeated the French and Spanish fleets at the Battle of Trafalgar. Admiral Nelson led the British fleet, but was killed in the battle.

4) In 1815, the Duke of Wellington defeated the French (led by the Emperor Napoleon) at the Battle of Waterloo.

The Union Flag

Although Ireland had had the same monarch as England and Wales since Henry VIII, it had remained a separate country. In 1801, Ireland became unified with England, Scotland and Wales after the Act of Union of 1800. This created the United Kingdom of Great Britain and Ireland. One symbol of this union between England, Scotland, Wales and Ireland was a new version of the official flag, the Union Flag. This is often called the Union Jack. The flag combined crosses associated with England, Scotland and Ireland. It is still used today as the official flag of the UK.

The Union Flag consists of three crosses:

The cross of St George, patron saint of England, is a red cross on a white ground.

St George's Cross of England

The cross of St Andrew, patron saint of Scotland, is a diagonal white cross on a blue ground.

St Andrew's Cross of Scotland

The cross of St Patrick, patron saint of Ireland, is a diagonal red cross on a white ground.

St Patrick's Cross of Ireland

Union Flag of the UK

There is also an official Welsh flag, which shows a Welsh dragon. The Welsh dragon does not appear on the Union Flag because, when the first Union Flag was created in 1606 from the flags of Scotland and England, the Principality of Wales was already united with England.

The official Welsh flag

1) Ireland had been ruled by the same monarch as England and Wales since Henry VIII, but it was a separate country.

2) After the Act of Union of 1800, Ireland was unified with England, Scotland and Wales in 1801.

3) The Act of Union created the United Kingdom of Great Britain and Ireland.

4) The Union Flag (also known as the Union Jack) is made up of the flags of England, Scotland and Ireland.

5) When the Union Flag was created in 1606, Wales was already united with England — so the Welsh dragon does not appear on it.

The Victorian Age

In 1837, Queen Victoria became queen of the UK at the age of 18. She reigned until 1901, almost 64 years. At the date of writing (2013) this is the longest reign of any British monarch. Her reign is known as the Victorian Age. It was a time when Britain increased in power and influence abroad. Within the UK, the middle classes became increasingly significant and a number of reformers led moves to improve conditions of life for the poor.

The British Empire

During the Victorian period, the British Empire grew to cover all of India, Australia and large parts of Africa. It became the largest empire the world has ever seen, with an estimated population of more than 400 million people.

Many people were encouraged to leave the UK to settle overseas. Between 1853 and 1913, as many as 13 million British citizens left the country. People continued to come to Britain from other parts of the world. For example, between 1870 and 1914, around 120,000 Russian and Polish Jews came to Britain to escape persecution. Many settled in London's East End and in Manchester and Leeds. People from the Empire, including India and Africa, also came to Britain to live, work and study.

1) Queen Victoria reigned until 1901 — nearly 64 years. This is the longest reign of any British monarch to date.

2) During the Victorian Age, the British Empire became the largest empire the world has ever seen.

3) It had a population of more than 400 million people.

4) Between 1853 and 1913, approximately 13 million British people moved overseas.

5) Between 1870 and 1914, about 120,000 Russian and Polish Jews moved to Britain to avoid persecution.

©iStockphoto.com/Duncan Walker

Queen Victoria came to the throne in 1837, when she was 18

Trade and industry

❝Britain continued to be a great trading nation. The government began to promote policies of free trade, abolishing a number of taxes on imported goods. One example of this was the repealing of the Corn Laws in 1846. These had prevented the import of cheap grain. The reforms helped the development of British industry, because raw materials could now be imported more cheaply.

Working conditions in factories gradually became better. In 1847, the number of hours that women and children could work was limited by law to 10 hours per day. Better housing began to be built for workers.

Transport links also improved, enabling goods and people to move more easily around the country. Just before Victoria came to the throne, the father and son George and Robert Stephenson pioneered the railway engine and a major expansion of the railways took place in the Victorian period. Railways were built throughout the Empire. There were also great advances in other areas, such as the building of bridges by engineers such as Isambard Kingdom Brunel.

Isambard Kingdom Brunel (1806-59)

Brunel was originally from Portsmouth, England. He was an engineer who built tunnels, bridges, railway lines and ships. He was responsible for constructing the Great Western Railway, which was the first major railway built in Britain. It runs from Paddington Station in London to the south west of England, the West Midlands and Wales. Many of Brunel's bridges are still in use today.

British industry led the world in the 19th century. The UK produced more than half of the world's iron, coal and cotton cloth. The UK also became a centre for financial services, including insurance and banking. In 1851, the Great Exhibition opened in Hyde Park in the Crystal Palace, a huge building made of steel and glass. Exhibits ranged from huge machines to handmade goods. Countries from all over the world showed their goods but most of the objects were made in Britain.

1) The government abolished taxes on some imported goods. This helped British industry develop by allowing cheap imports of raw materials.

2) The repealing (cancellation) of the Corn Laws in 1846 meant that cheap grain could be imported.

3) Just before Victoria's reign, George and Robert Stephenson pioneered the railway engine.

4) The engineer Isambard Kingdom Brunel built railways, ships, and many bridges that are still used today.

Isambard Kingdom Brunel designed the Clifton Suspension Bridge, which spans the Avon Gorge

©iStockphoto.com/krzych-34

5) In the 19th century, Britain produced much of the world's iron and coal, and became a centre for financial services.

6) In 1851, the Great Exhibition was held in the Crystal Palace. Most of the things on display were made in Britain.

The Crimean War

From 1853 to 1856, Britain fought with Turkey and France against Russia in the Crimean War. It was the first war to be extensively covered by the media through news stories and photographs. The conditions were very poor and many soldiers died from illnesses they caught in the hospitals, rather than from war wounds. Queen Victoria introduced the Victoria Cross medal during this war. It honours acts of valour by soldiers.

Florence Nightingale (1820-1910)

Florence Nightingale was born in Italy to English parents. At the age of 31, she trained as a nurse in Germany. In 1854, she went to Turkey and worked in military hospitals, treating soldiers who were fighting in the Crimean War. She and her fellow nurses improved the conditions in the hospital and reduced the mortality rate. In 1860 she established the Nightingale Training School for nurses at St Thomas' Hospital in London. The school was the first of its kind and still exists today, as do many of the practices that Florence used. She is often regarded as the founder of modern nursing.

Florence Nightingale was a nurse in Turkey during the Crimean War

Ireland in the 19th century

Conditions in Ireland were not as good as in the rest of the UK. Two-thirds of the population still depended on farming to make their living, often on very small plots of land. Many depended on potatoes as a large part of their diet. In the middle of the century the potato crop failed, and Ireland suffered a famine. A million people died from disease and starvation. Another million and a half left Ireland. Some emigrated to the United States and others came to England. By 1861 there were large populations of Irish people in cities such as Liverpool, London, Manchester and Glasgow.

The Irish Nationalist movement had grown strongly through the 19th century. Some, such as the Fenians, favoured complete independence. Others, such as Charles Stuart Parnell, advocated 'Home Rule', in which Ireland would remain in the UK but have its own parliament.

1) In the Crimean War (1853-1856), Britain fought alongside Turkey and France against Russia.

2) During the war, many of the wounded soldiers died from illness because the conditions in the military hospitals were very poor.

3) In 1854, Florence Nightingale went to Turkey as a nurse and worked in the military hospitals.

4) She improved conditions in the hospitals and reduced the number of soldiers that died while they were being treated.

5) In the mid 19th century, the potato crop in Ireland failed — a million people died of starvation and disease in the famine.

6) Another million and a half left Ireland and many of them emigrated to England and the United States.

7) The Irish Nationalist movement grew in the 19th century.

8) The Fenians wanted complete independence for Ireland. Others, including Charles Stuart Parnell, argued for 'Home Rule' (where Ireland would stay in the UK, but have its own parliament).

The right to vote

❝ As the middle classes in the wealthy industrial towns and cities grew in influence, they began to demand more political power. The Reform Act of 1832 had greatly increased the number of people with the right to vote. The Act also abolished the old pocket and rotten boroughs (see page 33) and more parliamentary seats were given to the towns and cities. There was a permanent shift of political power from the countryside to the towns but voting was still based on ownership of property. This meant that members of the working class were still unable to vote.

A movement began to demand the vote for the working classes and other people without property. Campaigners, called the Chartists, presented petitions to Parliament. At first they seemed to be unsuccessful, but in 1867 there was another Reform Act. This created many more urban seats in Parliament and reduced the amount of property that people needed to have before they could vote. However, the majority of men still did not have the right to vote and no women could vote.

Politicians realised that the increased number of voters meant that they needed to persuade people to vote for them if they were to be sure of being elected to

Parliament. The political parties began to create organisations to reach out to ordinary voters. Universal suffrage (the right of every adult, male or female, to vote) followed in the next century.

In common with the rest of Europe, women in 19th century Britain had fewer rights than men. Until 1870, when a woman got married, her earnings, property and money automatically belonged to her husband. Acts of Parliament in 1870 and 1882 gave wives the right to keep their own earnings and property. In the late 19th and early 20th centuries, an increasing number of women campaigned and demonstrated for greater rights and, in particular, the right to vote. They formed the women's suffrage movement and became known as 'suffragettes'.

Emmeline Pankhurst (1858-1928)

Emmeline Pankhurst was born in Manchester in 1858. She set up the Women's Franchise League in 1889, which fought to get the vote in local elections for married women. In 1903 she helped found the Women's Social and Political Union (WSPU). This was the first group whose members were called 'suffragettes'. The group used civil disobedience as part of their protest to gain the vote for women. They chained themselves to railings, smashed windows and committed arson. Many of the women, including Emmeline, went on hunger strike. In 1918, women over the age of 30 were given voting rights and the right to stand for Parliament, partly in recognition of the contribution women made to the war effort during the First World War. Shortly before Emmeline's death in 1928, women were given the right to vote at the age of 21, the same as men.

Emmeline Pankhurst and other suffragettes campaigned for women's right to vote

1) The Reform Acts in 1832 and 1867 gave more people the vote, but most men still could not vote and no women could vote.

2) In 1903, Emmeline Pankhurst helped found the Women's Social and Political Union. Its members were called 'suffragettes'.

3) The suffragettes campaigned for women's rights, particularly the right to vote.

4) In 1918, women over 30 were given voting rights and the right to stand for Parliament.

5) In 1928, women got the right to vote at 21, the same age as men.

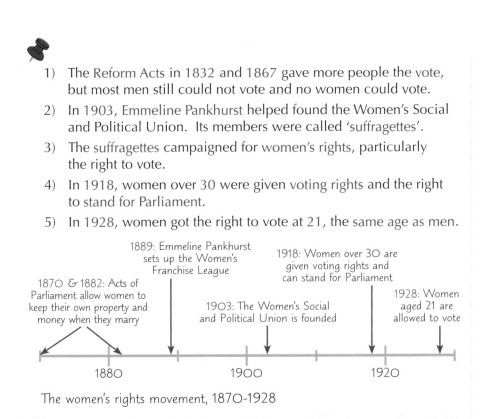

The women's rights movement, 1870-1928

The future of the Empire

66 Although the British Empire continued to grow until the 1920s, there was already discussion in the late 19th century about its future direction. Supporters of expansion believed that the Empire benefited Britain through increased trade and commerce. Others thought the Empire had become over-expanded and that the frequent conflicts in many parts of the Empire, such as India's north-west frontier or southern Africa, were a drain on resources. Yet the great majority of British people believed in the Empire as a force for good in the world.

The Boer War of 1899 to 1902 made the discussions about the future of the Empire more urgent. The British went to war in South Africa with settlers from the Netherlands called the Boers. The Boers fought fiercely and the war went on for over three years. Many died in the fighting and many more from disease. There was some public sympathy for the Boers and people began to question whether the Empire could continue. As different parts of the Empire developed, they won greater freedom and autonomy from Britain. Eventually, by the second half of the 20th century, there was, for the most part, an orderly transition from Empire to Commonwealth, with countries being granted their independence.

Rudyard Kipling (1865-1936)

Rudyard Kipling was born in India in 1865 and later lived in India, the UK and the USA. He wrote books and poems set in both India and the UK. His poems and novels reflected the idea that the British Empire was a force for good. Kipling was awarded the Nobel Prize in Literature in 1907. His books include the *Just So Stories* and *The Jungle Book*, which continue to be popular today. His poem *If* has often been voted among the UK's favourite poems. It begins with these words:

'If you can keep your head when all about you
Are losing theirs and blaming it on you;
If you can trust yourself when all men doubt you,
But make allowance for their doubting too;
If you can wait and not be tired by waiting,
Or being lied about, don't deal in lies,
Or being hated, don't give way to hating,
And yet don't look too good, nor talk too wise'

(*If*, Rudyard Kipling)

1) In South Africa, Britain fought settlers from the Netherlands in the Boer War (1899-1902).

2) The war divided public opinion about the future of the Empire.

3) As countries in the Empire developed, they were granted greater freedom from Britain.

4) The Empire gradually changed to become the Commonwealth as countries were granted their independence.

5) Rudyard Kipling won the Nobel Prize in Literature in 1907. His poem *If* is among the UK's favourite poems.

The 20th century

The First World War

66 The early 20th century was a time of optimism in Britain. The nation, with its expansive Empire, well-admired navy, thriving industry and strong political institutions, was what is now known as a global 'superpower'. It was also a time of social progress. Financial help for the unemployed, old-age pensions and free school meals were just a few of the important measures introduced. Various laws were passed to improve safety in the workplace; town planning rules were tightened to prevent the further development of slums; and better support was given to mothers and their children after divorce or separation. Local government became more democratic and a salary for members of Parliament (MPs) was introduced for the first time, making it easier for more people to take part in public life.

This era of optimism and progress was cut short when war broke out between several European nations. On 28 June 1914, Archduke Franz Ferdinand of Austria was assassinated. This set off a chain of events leading to the First World War (1914-18). But while the assassination provided the trigger for war, other factors — such as a growing sense of nationalism in many European states; increasing militarism; imperialism; and the division of the major European powers into two camps — all set the conditions for war.

The conflict was centred in Europe, but it was a global war involving nations from around the world. Britain was part of the Allied Powers, which included (amongst others) France, Russia, Japan, Belgium, Serbia — and later, Greece, Italy, Romania and the United States. The whole of the British Empire was involved in the conflict — for example, more than a million Indians fought on behalf of Britain in lots of different countries, and around 40,000 were killed. Men from the West Indies, Africa, Australia, New Zealand and Canada also fought with the British. The Allies fought against the Central Powers — mainly Germany, the Austro-Hungarian Empire, the Ottoman Empire and later Bulgaria. Millions of people were killed or wounded, with more than 2 million British casualties. One battle, the British attack on the Somme in July 1916, resulted in about 60,000 British casualties on the first day alone.

The First World War ended at 11.00 am on 11th November 1918 with victory for Britain and its allies. 99

1) In the early 20th century, financial help for the unemployed, old-age pensions and free school meals were introduced.

2) For the first time a salary was introduced for MPs, making it easier for more people to take part in public life.

3) The assassination of Archduke Franz Ferdinand was the trigger for the First World War (1914-1918).

4) Britain and the other Allied Powers (including France and Russia) fought against the Central Powers (mainly Germany, the Austro-Hungarian Empire and the Ottoman Empire).

5) Soldiers from the whole of the British Empire fought with Britain.

6) At 11.00 am on 11th November 1918, the war ended with victory for Britain and its allies.

©iStockphoto.com/stockcam

There were over 2 million British casualties during the First World War

The partition of Ireland

❝❝ In 1913, the British government promised 'Home Rule' for Ireland. The proposal was to have a self-governing Ireland with its own parliament but still part of the UK. A Home Rule Bill was introduced in Parliament. It was opposed by the Protestants in the north of Ireland, who threatened to resist Home Rule by force.

The outbreak of the First World War led the British government to postpone any changes in Ireland. Irish Nationalists were not willing to wait and in 1916 there was an uprising (the Easter Rising) against the British in Dublin. The leaders of the uprising were executed under military law. A guerrilla war against the British army and the police in Ireland followed. In 1921 a peace treaty was signed and in 1922 Ireland became two countries. The six counties in the north which were mainly Protestant remained part of the UK under the name Northern Ireland. The rest of Ireland became the Irish Free State. It had its own government and became a republic in 1949.

There were people in both parts of Ireland who disagreed with the split between the North and the South. They still wanted Ireland to be one independent country. Years of disagreement led to a terror campaign in Northern Ireland and elsewhere. The conflict between those wishing for full Irish independence and those wishing to remain loyal to the British government is often referred to as 'the Troubles'. 99

1) In 1913, Britain proposed 'Home Rule' for Ireland. 'Home Rule' was opposed by Protestants in the north of Ireland.

2) The Easter Rising in 1916 saw Irish Nationalists rise up against the British in Dublin.

3) The uprising led to a conflict in which the Nationalists fought the British army and the police in Ireland.

4) A peace treaty was signed in 1921, and Ireland became two countries (Northern Ireland and the Irish Free State) in 1922.

5) The fighting between those who wanted full Irish independence and those who wanted to remain loyal to the British government continued. This is known as 'the Troubles'.

The partition of Ireland, 1913-1949

The inter-war period

66 In the 1920s, many people's living conditions got better. There were improvements in public housing and new homes were built in many towns and cities. However, in 1929, the world entered the 'Great Depression' and some parts of the UK suffered mass unemployment. The effects of the depression of the 1930s were felt differently in different parts of the UK. The traditional heavy industries such as shipbuilding were badly affected but new industries — including the automobile and aviation industries — developed. As prices

generally fell, those in work had more money to spend. Car ownership doubled from 1 million to 2 million between 1930 and 1939. In addition, many new houses were built. It was also a time of cultural blossoming, with writers such as Graham Greene and Evelyn Waugh prominent. The economist John Maynard Keynes published influential new theories of economics. The BBC started radio broadcasts in 1922 and began the world's first regular television service in 1936. ""

1) In the 1920s, living conditions improved for many people.

2) In 1929, the 'Great Depression' caused mass unemployment in some parts of the UK.

3) In the 1930s, traditional heavy industries began to suffer, but new industries (such as the aviation industry) developed.

4) Graham Greene and Evelyn Waugh were prominent writers in the inter-war period.

5) The BBC began radio broadcasts in 1922 and the world's first regular television service in 1936.

The Second World War

""Adolf Hitler came to power in Germany in 1933. He believed that the conditions imposed on Germany by the Allies after the First World War were unfair; he also wanted to conquer more land for the German people. He set about renegotiating treaties, building up arms, and testing Germany's military strength in nearby countries. The British government tried to avoid another war. However, when Hitler invaded Poland in 1939, Britain and France declared war in order to stop his aggression.

The war was initially fought between the Axis powers (fascist Germany and Italy and the Empire of Japan) and the Allies. The main countries on the allied side were the UK, France, Poland, Australia, New Zealand, Canada, and the Union of South Africa.

Having occupied Austria and invaded Czechoslovakia, Hitler followed his invasion of Poland by taking control of Belgium and the Netherlands. Then, in 1940, German forces defeated allied troops and advanced through France. At this time of national crisis, Winston Churchill became Prime Minister and Britain's war leader.

Winston Churchill (1874-1965)

Churchill was the son of a politician and, before becoming a Conservative MP in 1900, was a soldier and journalist. In May 1940 he became Prime Minister. He refused to surrender to the Nazis and was an inspirational leader to the British people in a time of great hardship. He lost the General Election in 1945 but returned as Prime Minister in 1951.

He was an MP until he stood down at the 1964 General Election. Following his death in 1965, he was given a state funeral. He remains a much-admired figure to this day, and in 2002 was voted the greatest Briton of all time by the public. During the War, he made many famous speeches including lines which you may still hear:

'I have nothing to offer but blood, toil, tears and sweat'
Churchill's first speech to the House of Commons after he became Prime Minister, 1940

**'We shall fight on the beaches,
we shall fight on the landing grounds,
we shall fight in the fields and in the streets,
we shall fight in the hills;
we shall never surrender'**
Speech to the House of Commons after Dunkirk (see below), 1940

'Never in the field of human conflict was so much owed by so many to so few'
Speech to the House of Commons during the Battle of Britain (see below), 1940

Winston Churchill is famous for his inspirational leadership

As France fell, the British decided to evacuate British and French soldiers from France in a huge naval operation. Many civilian volunteers in small pleasure and fishing boats from Britain helped the Navy to rescue more than 300,000 men from the beaches around Dunkirk. Although many lives and a lot of equipment were lost, the evacuation was a success and meant that Britain was better able to continue the fight against the Germans. The evacuation gave rise to the phrase 'the Dunkirk spirit'.

From the end of June 1940 until the German invasion of the Soviet Union in June 1941, Britain and the Empire stood almost alone against Nazi Germany.

Hitler wanted to invade Britain, but before sending in troops, Germany needed to control the air. The Germans waged an air campaign against Britain, but the British resisted with their fighter planes and eventually won the crucial aerial battle against the Germans, called 'the Battle of Britain', in the summer of 1940. The most important planes, used by the Royal Air Force in the Battle of Britain were the Spitfire and the Hurricane — which were designed and built in Britain. Despite this crucial victory, the German air force was able to continue bombing London and other British cities at night-time. This was called the Blitz. Coventry was almost totally destroyed and a great deal of damage was done in other cities, especially in the East End of London. Despite the destruction, there was a strong national spirit of resistance in the UK. The phrase 'the Blitz spirit' is still used today to describe Britons pulling together in the face of adversity. 🙷

1) In 1939, Adolf Hitler invaded Poland. As a result, Britain and France declared war on Germany.

2) The Allies (including the UK) fought the Axis powers (including Germany, Italy and the Empire of Japan).

3) Winston Churchill became Britain's Prime Minister in 1940. He was an inspirational leader, and he refused to surrender to Germany.

4) In 1940, 300,000 British and French soldiers were evacuated from Dunkirk (France) in a huge naval operation.

5) The Royal Air Force won the 'Battle of Britain' in 1940, and stopped Hitler from invading Britain.

6) However, German planes continued to bomb British cities at night — this bombing campaign was called the Blitz.

66 At the same time as defending Britain, the British military was fighting the Axis on many other fronts. In Singapore, the Japanese defeated the British and then occupied Burma, threatening India. The United States entered the war when the Japanese bombed its naval base at Pearl Harbour in December 1941.

That same year, Hitler attempted the largest invasion in history by attacking the Soviet Union. It was a fierce conflict, with huge losses on both sides. German forces were ultimately repelled by the Soviets, and the damage they sustained proved to be a pivotal point in the war.

The allied forces gradually gained the upper hand, winning significant victories in North Africa and Italy. German losses in the Soviet Union, combined with the support of the Americans, meant that the Allies were eventually strong enough to attack Hitler's forces in Western Europe. On 6 June 1944, allied forces landed in Normandy (this event is often referred to as 'D-Day'). Following victory on the beaches of Normandy, the allied forces pressed on through France and eventually into Germany. The Allies comprehensively defeated Germany in May 1945.

The war against Japan ended in August 1945 when the United States dropped its newly developed atom bombs on the Japanese cities of Hiroshima and Nagasaki. Scientists led by Ernest Rutherford, working at Manchester and then Cambridge University, were the first to 'split the atom' and took part in the Manhattan Project in the United States, which developed the atomic bomb. The war was finally over.

Alexander Fleming (1881-1955)

Born in Scotland, Fleming moved to London as a teenager and later qualified as a doctor. He was researching influenza (the 'flu') in 1928 when he discovered penicillin. This was then further developed into a usable drug by the scientists Howard Florey and Ernst Chain. By the 1940s it was in mass production. Fleming won the Nobel Prize in Medicine in 1945. Penicillin is still used to treat bacterial infections today.

99

1) Britain fought in Asia as well as in Europe. The Japanese defeated the British in Singapore and occupied Burma.

2) In 1941, Hitler invaded the Soviet Union, and the United States entered the war after the Japanese attack on Pearl Harbour.

3) On 6 June 1944 (D-Day), allied forces landed in Normandy, France. They advanced through France and into Germany.

4) Germany was eventually defeated in May 1945.

5) In the east, the war against Japan ended when the United States dropped atomic bombs on Hiroshima and Nagasaki.

6) Ernest Rutherford's British team were the first to 'split the atom'. They were also involved in the Manhattan Project, which developed the atomic bomb.

7) Alexander Fleming discovered penicillin in 1928. Howard Florey and Ernst Chain developed it into a usable drug.

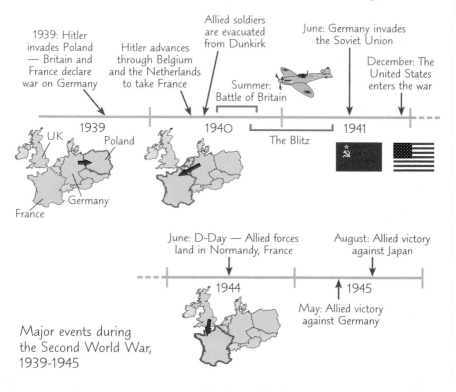

Major events during the Second World War, 1939-1945

Britain since 1945

The welfare state

“Although the UK had won the war, the country was exhausted economically and the people wanted change. During the war, there had been significant reforms to the education system and people now looked for wider social reforms.

In 1945 the British people elected a Labour government. The new Prime Minister was Clement Attlee, who promised to introduce the welfare state outlined in the Beveridge Report. In 1948, Aneurin (Nye) Bevan, the Minister for Health, led the establishment of the National Health Service (NHS), which guaranteed a minimum standard of health care for all, free at the point of use. A national system of benefits was also introduced to provide 'social security', so that the population would be protected from the 'cradle to the grave'. The government took into public ownership (nationalised) the railways, coal mines and gas, water and electricity supplies.

Another aspect of change was self-government for former colonies. In 1947, independence was granted to nine countries, including India, Pakistan and Ceylon (now Sri Lanka). Other colonies in Africa, the Caribbean and the Pacific achieved independence over the next 20 years.

The UK developed its own atomic bomb and joined the new North Atlantic Treaty Organization (NATO), an alliance of nations set up to resist the perceived threat of invasion by the Soviet Union and its allies.

Clement Attlee (1883-1967)

Clement Attlee was born in London in 1883. His father was a solicitor and, after studying at Oxford University, Attlee became a barrister. He gave this up to do social work in East London and eventually became a Labour MP. He was Winston Churchill's Deputy Prime Minister in the wartime coalition government and became Prime Minister after the Labour Party won the 1945 election. He was Prime Minister from 1945 to 1951 and led the Labour Party for 20 years. Attlee's government undertook the nationalisation of major industries (like coal and steel), created the National Health Service and implemented many of Beveridge's plans for a stronger welfare state. Attlee also introduced measures to improve the conditions of workers.

Britain had a Conservative government from 1951 to 1964. The 1950s were a period of economic recovery after the war and increasing prosperity for working people. The Prime Minister of the day, Harold Macmillan, was famous for his 'wind of change' speech about decolonisation and independence for the countries of the Empire.

William Beveridge (1879-1963)

William Beveridge (later Lord Beveridge) was a British economist and social reformer. He served briefly as a Liberal MP and was subsequently the leader of the Liberals in the House of Lords but is best known for the 1942 report *Social Insurance and Allied Services* (known as the Beveridge Report). The report was commissioned by the wartime government in 1941. It recommended that the government should find ways of fighting the five 'Giant Evils' of Want, Disease, Ignorance, Squalor and Idleness and provided the basis of the modern welfare state.

R A Butler (1902-82)

Richard Austen Butler (later Lord Butler) was born in 1902. He became a Conservative MP in 1923 and held several positions before becoming responsible for education in 1941. In this role, he oversaw the introduction of the Education Act 1944 (often called 'The Butler Act'), which introduced free secondary education in England and Wales. The education system has changed significantly since the Act was introduced, but the division between primary and secondary schools that it enforced still remains in most areas of Britain.

Dylan Thomas (1914-53)

Dylan Thomas was a Welsh poet and writer. He often read and performed his work in public, including for the BBC. His most well-known works include the radio play *Under Milk Wood*, first performed after his death in 1954, and the poem *Do Not Go Gentle into That Good Night*, which he wrote for his dying father in 1952. He died at the age of 39 in New York. There are several memorials to him in his birthplace, Swansea, including a statue and the Dylan Thomas Centre.

1) In 1945, a Labour government was elected. The Prime Minister, Clement Attlee, promised to introduce the welfare state.

2) In 1948, the National Health Service (NHS) was established. The NHS provides health care for everyone.

3) 'Social security' benefits were also introduced, which aimed to protect people for their whole life (from the 'cradle to the grave').

4) In 1947, nine countries (including India, Pakistan and Ceylon — now Sri Lanka) were granted independence from Britain.

5) The UK had a Conservative government from 1951 to 1964.

6) In 1942, William Beveridge produced the Beveridge Report. The report stated that the government should fight the five 'Giant Evils' of Want, Disease, Ignorance, Squalor and Idleness.

7) R A Butler was responsible for the Education Act of 1944, which introduced free secondary education in England and Wales.

8) Dylan Thomas was a Welsh poet and writer. His works include *Under Milk Wood* and *Do Not Go Gentle into That Good Night*.

Migration in post-war Britain

❝ Rebuilding Britain after the Second World War was a huge task. There were labour shortages and the British government encouraged workers from Ireland and other parts of Europe to come to the UK and help with the reconstruction. In 1948, people from the West Indies were also invited to come and work.

During the 1950s, there was still a shortage of labour in the UK. Further immigration was therefore encouraged for economic reasons, and many industries advertised for workers from overseas. For example, centres were set up in the West Indies to recruit people to drive buses. Textile and engineering firms from the north of England and the Midlands sent agents to India and Pakistan to find workers. For about 25 years, people from the West Indies, India, Pakistan and (later) Bangladesh travelled to work and settle in Britain.

Social change in the 1960s

The decade of the 1960s was a period of significant social change. It was known as 'the Swinging Sixties'. There was growth in British fashion, cinema and popular music. Two well-known pop music groups at the time were The Beatles and The Rolling Stones. People started to become better off and many bought cars and other consumer goods.

It was also a time when social laws were liberalised, for example in relation to divorce and to abortion in England, Wales and Scotland. The position of women in the workplace also improved. It was quite common at the time for employers to ask women to leave their jobs when they got married, but Parliament passed new laws giving women the right to equal pay and made it illegal for employers to discriminate against women because of their gender.

The 1960s was also a time of technological progress. Britain and France developed the world's only supersonic commercial airliner, Concorde. New styles of architecture, including high-rise buildings and the use of concrete and steel, became common.

The number of people migrating from the West Indies, India, Pakistan and what is now Bangladesh fell in the late 1960s because the government passed new laws to restrict immigration to Britain. Immigrants were required to have a strong connection to Britain through birth or ancestry. Even so, during the early 1970s, Britain admitted 28,000 people of Indian origin who had been forced to leave Uganda.

1) After the war there was a shortage of workers in Britain.

2) The government encouraged people from Ireland, Europe, and (in 1948) the West Indies to come and work in Britain.

3) In the 1950s, people were recruited from India and Pakistan to work for textile and engineering firms.

4) In the 1960s, new laws made it illegal for employers to discriminate against women because of their gender.

5) Laws were passed in the late 1960s to restrict immigration to Britain. However, 28,000 people of Indian origin were admitted in the early 1970s after they were forced to leave Uganda.

66

Some great British inventions of the 20th century

Britain has given the world some wonderful inventions. Examples from the 20th century include:

The **television** was developed by Scotsman John Logie Baird (1888-1946) in the 1920s. In 1932 he made the first television broadcast between London and Glasgow.

Radar was developed by Scotsman Sir Robert Watson-Watt (1892-1973), who proposed that enemy aircraft could be detected by radio waves. The first successful radar test took place in 1935.

Working with radar led Sir Bernard Lovell (1913-2012) to make new discoveries in astronomy. The radio telescope he built at **Jodrell Bank** in Cheshire was for many years the biggest in the world and continues to operate today.

A **Turing machine** is a theoretical mathematical device invented by Alan Turing (1912-54), a British mathematician, in the 1930s. The theory was influential in the development of computer science and the modern-day computer.

The Scottish physician and researcher John Macleod (1876-1935) was the co-discoverer of **insulin**, used to treat diabetes.

The **structure of the DNA molecule** was discovered in 1953 through work at British universities in London and Cambridge. This discovery contributed to many scientific advances, particularly in medicine and fighting crime. Francis Crick (1916-2004), one of those awarded the Nobel Prize for this discovery, was British.

The **jet engine** was developed in Britain in the 1930s by Sir Frank Whittle (1907-96), a British Royal Air Force engineer officer.

Sir Christopher Cockerel (1910-99), a British inventor, invented the **hovercraft** in the 1950s.

Tip: Learn when these inventions and discoveries were made, and who made them.

Britain and France developed **Concorde**, the world's only supersonic passenger aircraft. It first flew in 1969 and began carrying passengers in 1976. Concorde was retired from service in 2003.

The **Harrier jump jet**, an aircraft capable of taking off vertically, was also designed and developed in the UK.

In the 1960s, James Goodfellow (1937-) invented the **cash-dispensing ATM** (automatic teller machine) or 'cashpoint'. The first of these was put into use by Barclays Bank in Enfield, north London in 1967.

IVF (in-vitro fertilisation) therapy for the treatment of infertility was pioneered in Britain by physiologist Sir Robert Edwards (1925-2013) and gynaecologist Patrick Steptoe (1913-88). The world's first 'test-tube baby' was born in Oldham, Lancashire in 1978.

In 1996, two British scientists, Sir Ian Wilmot (1944-) and Keith Campbell (1954-2012), led a team which was the first to succeed in **cloning** a mammal, Dolly the sheep. This has led to further research into the possible use of cloning to preserve endangered species and for medical purposes.

Sir Peter Mansfield (1933-), a British scientist, is the co-inventor of the **MRI (magnetic resonance imaging)** scanner. This enables doctors and researchers to obtain exact and non-invasive images of human internal organs and has revolutionised diagnostic medicine.

The inventor of the **World Wide Web**, Sir Tim Berners-Lee (1955-), is British. Information was successfully transferred via the web for the first time on 25 December 1990.

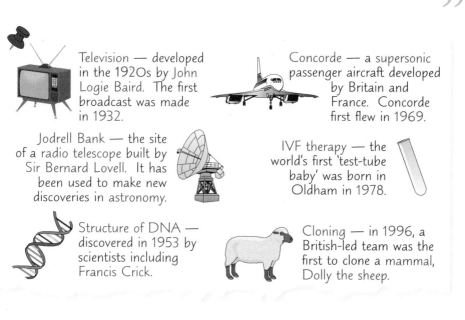

Television — developed in the 1920s by John Logie Baird. The first broadcast was made in 1932.

Concorde — a supersonic passenger aircraft developed by Britain and France. Concorde first flew in 1969.

Jodrell Bank — the site of a radio telescope built by Sir Bernard Lovell. It has been used to make new discoveries in astronomy.

IVF therapy — the world's first 'test-tube baby' was born in Oldham in 1978.

Structure of DNA — discovered in 1953 by scientists including Francis Crick.

Cloning — in 1996, a British-led team was the first to clone a mammal, Dolly the sheep.

Problems in the economy in the 1970s

66 In the late 1970s, the post-war economic boom came to an end. Prices of goods and raw materials began to rise sharply and the exchange rate between the pound and other currencies was unstable. This caused problems with the 'balance of payments': imports of goods were valued at more than the price paid for exports.

Many industries and services were affected by strikes and this caused problems between the trade unions and the government. People began to argue that the unions were too powerful and that their activities were harming the UK.

The 1970s were also a time of serious unrest in Northern Ireland. In 1972, the Northern Ireland Parliament was suspended and Northern Ireland was directly ruled by the UK government. Some 3,000 people lost their lives in the decades after 1969 in the violence in Northern Ireland.

Mary Peters (1939-)

Born in Manchester, Mary Peters moved to Northern Ireland as a child. She was a talented athlete who won an Olympic gold medal in the pentathlon in 1972. After this, she raised money for local athletics and became the team manager for the women's British Olympic team. She continues to promote sport and tourism in Northern Ireland and was made a Dame of the British Empire in 2000 in recognition of her work.

Europe and the Common Market

West Germany, France, Belgium, Italy, Luxembourg and the Netherlands formed the European Economic Community (EEC) in 1957. At first the UK did not wish to join the EEC but it eventually did so in 1973. The UK is a full member of the European Union but does not use the Euro currency.

Conservative government from 1979 to 1997

Margaret Thatcher, Britain's first woman Prime Minister, led the Conservative government from 1979 to 1990. The government made structural changes to the economy through the privatisation of nationalised industries and imposed legal controls on trade union powers. Deregulation saw a great increase in the role of the City of London as an international centre for investments, insurance and other financial services. Traditional industries, such as shipbuilding and coal mining, declined. In 1982, Argentina invaded the Falkland Islands, a British overseas territory in the South Atlantic. A naval taskforce was sent from the UK and military action led to the recovery of the islands.

John Major was Prime Minister after Mrs Thatcher, and helped establish the Northern Ireland peace process.

Margaret Thatcher (1925-2013)

Margaret Thatcher was the daughter of a grocer from Grantham in Lincolnshire. She trained as a chemist and lawyer. She was elected as a Conservative MP in 1959 and became a cabinet minister in 1970 as the Secretary of State for Education and Science. In 1975 she was elected as Leader of the Conservative Party and so became Leader of the Opposition.

Following the Conservative victory in the General Election in 1979, Margaret Thatcher became the first woman Prime Minister of the UK. She was the longest-serving Prime Minister of the 20th century, remaining in office until 1990.

During her premiership, there were a number of important economic reforms within the UK. She worked closely with the United States President, Ronald Reagan, and was one of the first Western leaders to recognise and welcome the changes in the leadership of the Soviet Union which eventually led to the end of the Cold War.

Margaret Thatcher worked closely with President Reagan

©Courtesy Everett Collection/ Rex Features

1) In the late 1970s Britain suffered from economic problems.

2) Widespread strikes caused problems between the trade unions and the government.

3) Serious unrest in Northern Ireland led to the Northern Ireland Parliament being suspended in 1972.

4) In 1972, Mary Peters won Olympic gold in the pentathlon.

5) In 1973, the UK joined the European Economic Community.

6) Margaret Thatcher became Britain's first woman Prime Minister.

7) She led the Conservative government from 1979 to 1990, and was the longest-serving Prime Minister of the 20th century.

8) In 1982, Argentina invaded the Falkland Islands. The UK fought the Argentinians, and the islands remained British.

Roald Dahl (1916-90)

Roald Dahl was born in Wales to Norwegian parents. He served in the Royal Air Force during the Second World War. It was during the 1940s that he began to publish books and short stories. He is most well known for his children's books, although he also wrote for adults. His best-known works include *Charlie and the Chocolate Factory* and *George's Marvellous Medicine*. Several of his books have been made into films.

Labour government from 1997 to 2010

In 1997 the Labour Party led by Tony Blair was elected. The Blair government introduced a Scottish Parliament and a Welsh Assembly (see page 117). The Scottish Parliament has substantial powers to legislate. The Welsh Assembly was given fewer legislative powers but considerable control over public services. In Northern Ireland, the Blair government was able to build on the peace process, resulting in the Good Friday Agreement signed in 1998. The Northern Ireland Assembly was elected in 1999 but suspended in 2002. It was not reinstated until 2007. Most paramilitary groups in Northern Ireland have decommissioned their arms and are inactive. Gordon Brown took over as Prime Minister in 2007.

Conflicts in Afghanistan and Iraq

Throughout the 1990s, Britain played a leading role in coalition forces involved in the liberation of Kuwait, following the Iraqi invasion in 1990, and the conflict in the Former Republic of Yugoslavia. Since 2000, British armed forces have been engaged in the global fight against international terrorism and against the proliferation of weapons of mass destruction, including operations in Afghanistan and Iraq. British combat troops left Iraq in 2009. The UK now operates in Afghanistan as part of the United Nations (UN) mandated 50-nation International Security Assistance Force (ISAF) coalition and at the invitation of the Afghan government. ISAF is working to ensure that Afghan territory can never again be used as a safe haven for international terrorism, where groups such as Al Qa'ida could plan attacks on the international community. As part of this, ISAF is building up the Afghan National Security Forces and is helping to create a secure environment in which governance and development can be extended. International forces are gradually handing over responsibility for security to the Afghans, who will have full security responsibility in all provinces by the end of 2014.

Coalition government 2010 onwards

In May 2010, and for the first time in the UK since February 1974, no political party won an overall majority in the General Election. The Conservative and Liberal Democrat parties formed a coalition and the leader of the Conservative Party, David Cameron, became Prime Minister. 99

1) The author, Roald Dahl, is best known for his children's books.

2) In 1997, the Labour Party was elected, with Tony Blair as leader.

3) The Blair government introduced the Scottish Parliament and the Welsh Assembly.

4) The peace process in Northern Ireland led to the Good Friday Agreement, which was signed in 1998.

5) In the 1990s, Britain was involved in the liberation of Kuwait and the conflict in the Former Republic of Yugoslavia.

6) Since 2000, British armed forces have been part of the fight against international terrorism. British troops have been involved in operations in Iraq and Afghanistan.

7) In 2010, the Conservative and Liberal Democrat parties formed a coalition, and David Cameron became Prime Minister.

A modern, thriving society

The UK today

❝ The UK today is a more diverse society than it was 100 years ago, in both ethnic and religious terms. Post-war immigration means that nearly 10% of the population has a parent or grandparent born outside the UK. The UK continues to be a multinational and multiracial society with a rich and varied culture. This section will tell you about the different parts of the UK and some of the important places. It will also explain some of the UK's traditions and customs and some of the popular activities that take place.

The nations of the UK

The UK is located in the north west of Europe. The longest distance on the mainland is from John O'Groats on the north coast of Scotland to Land's End in the south-west corner of England. It is about 870 miles (approximately 1,400 kilometres).

Most people live in towns and cities but much of Britain is still countryside. Many people continue to visit the countryside for holidays and for leisure activities such as walking, camping and fishing. ❞

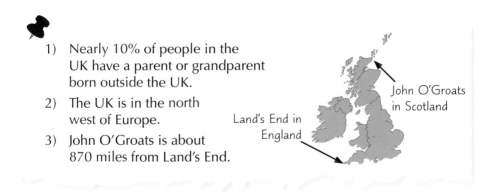

1) Nearly 10% of people in the UK have a parent or grandparent born outside the UK.

2) The UK is in the north west of Europe.

3) John O'Groats is about 870 miles from Land's End.

John O'Groats in Scotland

Land's End in England

UK currency

The currency in the UK is the pound sterling (symbol £). There are 100 pence in a pound. The denominations (values) of currency are:

- coins: 1p, 2p, 5p, 10p, 20p, 50p, £1 and £2
- notes: £5, £10, £20, £50.

Northern Ireland and Scotland have their own banknotes, which are valid everywhere in the UK. However, shops and businesses do not have to accept them.

Languages and dialects

There are many variations in language in the different parts of the UK. The English language has many accents and dialects. In Wales, many people speak Welsh — a completely different language from English — and it is taught in schools and universities. In Scotland, Gaelic (again, a different language) is spoken in some parts of the Highlands and Islands, and in Northern Ireland some people speak Irish Gaelic.

1) The UK currency is pound sterling (£). There are 100 pence (p) in one pound. These are the coins available:

| 1p | 2p | 5p | 10p | 20p | 50p | £1 | £2 |

2) Banknotes come in values of £5, £10, £20 and £50.

3) Northern Ireland and Scotland have their own banknotes.

4) Some people in the UK speak other languages as well as English — Welsh is spoken in Wales, Gaelic in the Scottish Highlands, and Irish Gaelic in Northern Ireland.

© Paul Rapson / Alamy

English banknotes

Population

66 The table below shows how the population of the UK has changed over time.

Population growth in the UK	
Year	**Population**
1600	Just over 4 million
1700	5 million
1801	8 million
1851	20 million
1901	40 million
1951	50 million
1998	57 million
2005	Just under 60 million
2010	Just over 62 million
Source: National Statistics	

Population growth has been faster in more recent years. Migration into the UK and longer life expectancy have played a part in population growth.

The population is very unequally distributed over the four parts of the UK. England more or less consistently makes up 84% of the total population, Wales around 5%, Scotland just over 8%, and Northern Ireland less than 3%.

An ageing population

People in the UK are living longer than ever before. This is due to improved living standards and better health care. There are now a record number of people aged 85 and over. This has an impact on the cost of pensions and health care.

Ethnic diversity

The UK population is ethnically diverse and changing rapidly, especially in large cities such as London. It is not always easy to get an exact picture of the ethnic origin of all the population.

There are people in the UK with ethnic origins from all over the world. In surveys, the most common ethnic description chosen is white, which includes people of European, Australian, Canadian, New Zealand and American descent. Other significant groups are those of Asian, black and mixed descent.

An equal society

Within the UK, it is a legal requirement that men and women should not be discriminated against because of their gender or because they are, or are not, married. They have equal rights to work, own property, marry and divorce. If they are married, both parents are equally responsible for their children.

Women in Britain today make up about half of the workforce. On average, girls leave school with better qualifications than boys. More women than men study at university.

Employment opportunities for women are much greater than they were in the past. Women work in all sectors of the economy, and there are now more women in high-level positions than ever before, including senior managers in traditionally male-dominated occupations. Alongside this, men now work in more varied jobs than they did in the past.

It is no longer expected that women should stay at home and not work. Women often continue to work after having children. In many families today, both partners work and both share responsibility for childcare and household chores. 99

1) The UK population has grown from just over 4 million in 1600, to just over 62 million in 2010.

2) The UK's population is unevenly distributed. The pie chart shows the percentage of the population living in each country:

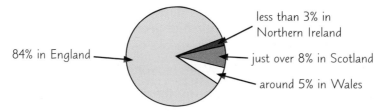

84% in England

less than 3% in Northern Ireland

just over 8% in Scotland

around 5% in Wales

3) The largest ethnic group in the UK is white. There are also large numbers of people of Asian, black and mixed descent.

4) Men and women have equal rights under UK law.

5) Women make up half of Britain's workforce.

6) Many women continue to work after having children.

Religion

❝ The UK is historically a Christian country. In the 2009 Citizenship Survey, 70% of people identified themselves as Christian. Much smaller proportions identified themselves as Muslim (4%), Hindu (2%), Sikh (1%), Jewish or Buddhist (both less than 0.5%), and 2% of people followed another religion. There are religious buildings for other religions all over the UK. This includes Islamic mosques, Hindu temples, Jewish synagogues, Sikh gurdwaras and Buddhist temples. However, everyone has the legal right to choose their religion, or to choose not to practise a religion. In the Citizenship Survey, 21% of people said that they had no religion.

Christian churches

In England, there is a constitutional link between Church and state. The official Church of the state is the Church of England (called the Anglican Church in other countries and the Episcopal Church in Scotland and the United States). It is a Protestant Church and has existed since the Reformation in the 1530s (see page 23 for an explanation).

The monarch is the head of the Church of England. The spiritual leader of the Church of England is the Archbishop of Canterbury. The monarch has the right to select the Archbishop and other senior church officials, but usually the choice is made by the Prime Minister and a committee appointed by the Church. Several Church of England bishops sit in the House of Lords (see page 110).

In Scotland, the national Church is the Church of Scotland, which is a Presbyterian Church. It is governed by ministers and elders. The chairperson of the General Assembly of the Church of Scotland is the Moderator, who is appointed for one year only and often speaks on behalf of that Church.

There is no established Church in Wales or Northern Ireland.

Other Protestant Christian groups in the UK are Baptists, Methodists, Presbyterians and Quakers. There are also other denominations of Christianity, the biggest of which is Roman Catholic.

Patron saints' days

England, Scotland, Wales and Northern Ireland each have a national saint, called a patron saint. Each saint has a special day:

- 1 March: St David's Day, Wales
- 17 March: St Patrick's Day, Northern Ireland

- 23 April: St George's Day, England

- 30 November: St Andrew's Day, Scotland.

Only Scotland and Northern Ireland have their patron saint's day as an official holiday (although in Scotland not all businesses and offices will close). Events are held across Scotland, Northern Ireland and the rest of the country, especially where there are a lot of people of Scottish, Northern Irish and Irish heritage.

While the patron saints' days are no longer public holidays in England and Wales, they are still celebrated. Parades and small festivals are held all over the two countries. 🍃🍃

1) The UK is historically a Christian country.
Today British people belong to many different religions:

Religion	% of people	Religion	% of people
Christian	70%	Jewish	Less than 0.5%
Muslim	4%	Buddhist	Less than 0.5%
Hindu	2%	Other	2%
Sikh	1%	No religion	21%

Source: 2009 Citizenship Survey

2) The Church of England is the official Church of the state in England. It is a Protestant Church which formed during the Reformation.

3) The monarch is the head of the Church of England, but the Archbishop of Canterbury is its spiritual leader.

4) The Church of Scotland is a Presbyterian Church. Its General Assembly is run by a Moderator who is appointed each year.

5) The patron saints are: St David for Wales, St Patrick for Northern Ireland, St George for England and St Andrew for Scotland.

Monarchs have been crowned in Westminster Abbey since 1066. 17 kings and queens are buried there.

Customs and traditions

The main Christian festivals

66 **Christmas Day**, 25 December, celebrates the birth of Jesus Christ. It is a public holiday. Many Christians go to church on Christmas Eve (24 December) or on Christmas Day itself.

Christmas is celebrated in a traditional way. People usually spend the day at home and eat a special meal, which often includes roast turkey, Christmas pudding and mince pies. They give gifts, send cards and decorate their houses. Christmas is a special time for children. Very young children believe that Father Christmas (also known as Santa Claus) brings them presents during the night before Christmas Day. Many people decorate a tree in their home.

Boxing Day is the day after Christmas Day and is a public holiday.

Easter takes place in March or April. It marks the death of Jesus Christ on Good Friday and his rising from the dead on Easter Sunday. Both Good Friday and the following Monday, called Easter Monday, are public holidays.

The 40 days before Easter are known as Lent. It is a time when Christians take time to reflect and prepare for Easter. Traditionally, people would fast during this period and today many people will give something up, like a favourite food. The day before Lent starts is called Shrove Tuesday, or Pancake Day. People eat pancakes, which were traditionally made to use up foods such as eggs, fat and milk before fasting. Lent begins on Ash Wednesday. There are church services where Christians are marked with an ash cross on their forehead as a symbol of death and sorrow for sin.

Easter is also celebrated by people who are not religious. 'Easter eggs' are chocolate eggs often given as presents at Easter as a symbol of new life.

Other religious festivals

Tip: Look at page 147 for a summary of the important dates in the British calendar.

Diwali normally falls in October or November and lasts for five days. It is often called the Festival of Lights. It is celebrated by Hindus and Sikhs. It celebrates the victory of good over evil and the gaining of knowledge. There are different stories about how the festival came about. There is a famous celebration of Diwali in Leicester.

Hannukah is in November or December and is celebrated for eight days. It is to remember the Jews' struggle for religious freedom. On each day of the festival a candle is lit on a stand of eight candles (called a menorah) to remember the story of the festival, where oil that should have lasted only a day did so for eight.

Eid al-Fitr celebrates the end of Ramadan, when Muslims have fasted for a month. They thank Allah for giving them the strength to complete the fast. The date when it takes place changes every year. Muslims attend special services and meals.

Eid ul Adha remembers that the prophet Ibrahim was willing to sacrifice his son when God ordered him to. It reminds Muslims of their own commitment to God. Many Muslims sacrifice an animal to eat during this festival. In Britain this has to be done in a slaughterhouse.

Vaisakhi (also spelled Baisakhi) is a Sikh festival which celebrates the founding of the Sikh community known as the Khalsa. It is celebrated on 14 April each year with parades, dancing and singing.

Other festivals and traditions

New Year, 1 January, is a public holiday. People usually celebrate on the night of 31 December (called New Year's Eve). In Scotland, 31 December is called Hogmanay and 2 January is also a public holiday. For some Scottish people, Hogmanay is a bigger holiday than Christmas.

Valentine's Day, 14 February, is when lovers exchange cards and gifts. Sometimes people send anonymous cards to someone they secretly admire.

April Fool's Day, 1 April, is a day when people play jokes on each other until midday. The television and newspapers often have stories that are April Fool jokes.

Mothering Sunday (or Mother's Day) is the Sunday three weeks before Easter. Children send cards or buy gifts for their mothers.

Father's Day is the third Sunday in June. Children send cards or buy gifts for their fathers.

Halloween, 31 October, is an ancient festival and has roots in the pagan festival to mark the beginning of winter. Young people will often dress up in frightening costumes to play 'trick or treat'. People give them treats to stop them playing tricks on them. A lot of people carve lanterns out of pumpkins and put a candle inside.

Bonfire Night, 5 November, is an occasion when people in Great Britain set off fireworks at home or in special displays. The origin of this celebration was an event in 1605, when a group of Catholics led by Guy Fawkes failed in their plan to kill the Protestant king with a bomb in the Houses of Parliament.

Remembrance Day, 11 November, commemorates those who died fighting for the UK and its allies. Originally it commemorated the dead of the First World War, which ended on 11 November 1918. People wear poppies (the red flower found on the battlefields of the First World War). At 11.00 am there is a two-minute silence and wreaths are laid at the Cenotaph in Whitehall, London.

Bank holidays

As well as those mentioned previously, there are other public holidays each year called bank holidays, when banks and many other businesses are closed for the day. These are of no religious significance. They are at the beginning of May, in late May or early June, and in August. In Northern Ireland, the anniversary of the Battle of the Boyne in July is also a public holiday. 〟

1) The main Christian festivals are Christmas (25 December) and Easter (March or April).

2) Diwali, Hannukah, Eid al-Fitr, Eid ul Adha and Vaisakhi are important festivals celebrated by other religious groups in the UK.

3) Other well-known festivals include:

   • New Year's Eve / Hogmanay — 31 December

   • New Year — 1 January

   • Valentine's Day — 14 February

   • April Fool's Day — 1 April

   • Bonfire Night — 5 November

   • Remembrance Day — 11 November

©iStockphoto.com/JOHN GOMEZ

The Cenotaph in London was built in 1920. It is the focal-point of the Remembrance Day service.

4) Bank holidays are non-religious public holidays when many businesses close for the day.

Sport

❝ Sports of all kinds play an important part in many people's lives. There are several sports that are particularly popular in the UK. Many sporting events take place at major stadiums such as Wembley Stadium in London and the Millennium Stadium in Cardiff.

Local governments and private companies provide sports facilities such as swimming pools, tennis courts, football pitches, dry ski slopes and gymnasiums. Many famous sports, including cricket, football, lawn tennis, golf and rugby, began in Britain.

The UK has hosted the Olympic Games on three occasions: 1908, 1948 and 2012. The main Olympic site for the 2012 Games was in Stratford, East London. The British team was very successful, across a wide range of Olympic sports, finishing third in the medal table.

The Paralympic Games for 2012 were also hosted in London. The Paralympics have their origin in the work of Dr Sir Ludwig Guttman, a German refugee, at the Stoke Mandeville hospital in Buckinghamshire. Dr Guttman developed new methods of treatment for people with spinal injuries and encouraged patients to take part in exercise and sport.

Notable British sportsmen and women

Sir Roger Bannister (1929-) was the first man in the world to run a mile in under four minutes, in 1954.

Sir Jackie Stewart (1939-) is a Scottish former racing driver who won the Formula 1 world championship three times.

Bobby Moore (1941-93) captained the English football team that won the World Cup in 1966.

Sir Ian Botham (1955-) captained the English cricket team and holds a number of English Test cricket records, both for batting and for bowling.

Jayne Torvill (1957-) and Christopher Dean (1958-) won gold medals for ice dancing at the Olympic Games in 1984 and in four consecutive world championships.

Sir Steve Redgrave (1962-) won gold medals in rowing in five consecutive Olympic Games and is one of Britain's greatest Olympians.

Baroness Tanni Grey-Thompson (1969-) is an athlete who uses a wheelchair and won 16 Paralympic medals, including 11 gold medals, in races over five Paralympic Games. She won the London Marathon six times and broke a total of 30 world records.

Dame Kelly Holmes (1970-) won two gold medals for running in the 2004 Olympic Games. She has held a number of British and European records.

Dame Ellen MacArthur (1976-) is a yachtswoman and in 2004 became the fastest person to sail around the world singlehanded.

Sir Chris Hoy (1976-) is a Scottish cyclist who has won six gold and one silver Olympic medals. He has also won 11 world championship titles.

David Weir (1979-) is a Paralympian who uses a wheelchair and has won six gold medals over two Paralympic Games. He has also won the London Marathon six times.

Tip: Don't just learn the name of each sports person — learn their achievements too.

Bradley Wiggins (1980-) is a cyclist. In 2012, he became the first Briton to win the Tour de France. He has won seven Olympic medals, including gold medals in the 2004, 2008 and 2012 Olympic Games.

Mo Farah (1983-) is a British distance runner, born in Somalia. He won gold medals in the 2012 Olympics for the 5,000 and 10,000 metres and is the first Briton to win the Olympic gold medal in the 10,000 metres.

Jessica Ennis (1986-) is an athlete. She won the 2012 Olympic gold medal in the heptathlon, which includes seven different track and field events. She also holds a number of British athletics records.

Andy Murray (1987-) is a Scottish tennis player who in 2012 won the men's singles in the US Open. He is the first British man to win a singles title in a Grand Slam tournament since 1936. In the same year, he won Olympic gold and silver medals and was runner-up in the men's singles at Wimbledon (see page 82).

Ellie Simmonds (1994-) is a Paralympian who won gold medals for swimming at the 2008 and 2012 Paralympic Games and holds a number of world records. She was the youngest member of the British team at the 2008 Games.

1) Major sporting events are held at stadiums such as Wembley Stadium in London, and the Millennium Stadium in Cardiff.

2) The UK hosted the Olympics in 1908, 1948 and 2012.

3) Britain came third in the medal table at the 2012 Olympics.

4) The Paralympic games started in the UK from the work of Dr Sir Ludwig Guttman.

Golf is one of many famous sports that began in Britain

Cricket

Cricket originated in England and is now played in many countries. Games can last up to five days but still result in a draw! The idiosyncratic nature of the game and its complex laws are said to reflect the best of the British character and sense of fair play. You may come across expressions such as 'rain stopped play', 'batting on a sticky wicket', 'playing a straight bat', 'bowled a googly' or 'it's just not cricket', which have passed into everyday usage. The most famous competition is the Ashes, which is a series of Test matches played between England and Australia.

Football

Football is the UK's most popular sport. It has a long history in the UK and the first professional football clubs were formed in the late 19th century.

England, Scotland, Wales and Northern Ireland each have separate leagues in which clubs representing different towns and cities compete. The English Premier League attracts a huge international audience. Many of the best players in the world play in the Premier League. Many UK teams also compete in competitions such as the UEFA (Union of European Football Associations) Champions League, against other teams from Europe. Most towns and cities have a professional club and people take great pride in supporting their home team. There can be great rivalry between different football clubs and among fans.

Each country in the UK also has its own national team that competes with other national teams across the world in tournaments such as the FIFA (Fédération Internationale de Football Association) World Cup and the UEFA European Football Championships. England's only international tournament victory was at the World Cup of 1966, hosted in the UK.

Football is also a popular sport to play in many local communities, with people playing amateur games every week in parks all over the UK.

Rugby

Rugby originated in England in the early 19th century and is very popular in the UK today. There are two different types of rugby, which have different rules: union and league. Both have separate leagues and national teams in England, Wales, Scotland and Northern Ireland (who play with the Irish Republic). Teams from all countries compete in a range of competitions. The most famous rugby union competition is the Six Nations Championship between England, Ireland, Scotland, Wales, France and Italy. The Super League is the most well-known rugby league (club) competition.

Horse racing

There is a very long history of horse racing in Britain, with evidence of events taking place as far back as Roman times. The sport has a long association with royalty. There are racecourses all over the UK. Famous horse-racing events include: Royal Ascot, a five-day race meeting in Berkshire attended by members of the Royal Family; the Grand National at Aintree near Liverpool; and the Scottish Grand National at Ayr. There is a National Horseracing Museum in Newmarket, Suffolk.

Golf

The modern game of golf can be traced back to 15th century Scotland. It is a popular sport played socially as well as professionally. There are public and private golf courses all over the UK. St Andrews in Scotland is known as the home of golf. The Open Championship is the only 'Major' tournament held outside the United States. It is hosted by a different golf course every year.

Tennis

Modern tennis evolved in England in the late 19th century. The first tennis club was founded in Leamington Spa in 1872. The most famous tournament hosted in Britain is The Wimbledon Championships, which takes place each year at the All England Lawn Tennis and Croquet Club. It is the oldest tennis tournament in the world and the only 'Grand Slam' event played on grass.

Water sports

Sailing continues to be popular in the UK, reflecting our maritime heritage. A British sailor, Sir Francis Chichester, was the first person to sail single-handed around the world, in 1966/67. Two years later, Sir Robin Knox-Johnston became the first person to do this without stopping. Many sailing events are held throughout the UK, the most famous of which is at Cowes on the Isle of Wight.

Rowing is also popular, both as a leisure activity and as a competitive sport. There is a popular yearly race on the Thames between Oxford and Cambridge Universities.

Motor sports

There is a long history of motor sport in the UK, for both cars and motor cycles. Motor-car racing in the UK started in 1902. The UK continues to be a world leader in the development and manufacture of motor-sport technology. A Formula 1 Grand Prix event is held in the UK each year and a number of British Grand Prix drivers have won the Formula 1 World Championship. Recent British winners include Damon Hill, Lewis Hamilton and Jenson Button.

Skiing

Skiing is increasingly popular in the UK. Many people go abroad to ski and there are also dry ski slopes throughout the UK. Skiing on snow may also be possible during the winter. There are five ski centres in Scotland, as well as Europe's longest dry ski slope near Edinburgh.

1) Cricket originated in England. The most famous cricket competition is the Ashes between England and Australia.

2) Football is the UK's most popular sport.

3) Each country in the UK has a national football team.

4) England have won the FIFA World Cup once — in 1966.

5) The Six Nations is the most well-known rugby union competition that UK teams compete in. The Super League is the most famous rugby league (club) competition.

6) UK horse racing events include Royal Ascot, the Grand National and the Scottish Grand National.

7) The Open Championship is a 'Major' golf tournament held in the UK each year.

8) The Wimbledon Championships is the biggest tennis tournament in Britain.

9) An annual rowing race takes place on the Thames between Oxford and Cambridge Universities.

10) A Formula 1 Grand Prix car-racing event is held in the UK each year.

11) A number of British motorists, such as Jenson Button, have won the Formula 1 World Championship.

Arts and culture
Music

❝ Music is an important part of British culture, with a rich and varied heritage. It ranges from classical music to modern pop. There are many different venues and musical events that take place across the UK.

The Proms is an eight-week summer season of orchestral classical music that takes place in various venues, including the Royal Albert Hall in London. It has been organised by the British Broadcasting Corporation (BBC) since 1927. The Last Night of the Proms is the most well-known concert and (along with others in the series) is broadcast on television.

Classical music has been popular in the UK for many centuries. **Henry Purcell (1659-95)** was the organist at Westminster Abbey. He wrote church music, operas and other pieces, and developed a British style distinct from that elsewhere in Europe. He continues to be influential on British composers.

The German-born composer **George Frederick Handel (1695-1759)** spent many years in the UK and became a British citizen in 1727. He wrote the *Water Music* for King George I and *Music for the Royal Fireworks* for his son, George II. Both these pieces continue to be very popular. Handel also wrote an oratorio, *Messiah*, which is sung regularly by choirs, often at Easter time.

More recently, important composers include **Gustav Holst (1874-1934)**, whose work includes *The Planets*, a suite of pieces themed around the planets of the solar system. He adapted *Jupiter*, part of the *Planets* suite, as the tune for *I vow to thee my country*, a popular hymn in British churches.

Sir Edward Elgar (1857-1934) was born in Worcester, England. His best-known work is probably the *Pomp and Circumstance Marches*. *March No 1 (Land of Hope and Glory)* is usually played at the Last Night of the Proms at the Royal Albert Hall.

Ralph Vaughan Williams (1872-1958) wrote music for orchestras and choirs. He was strongly influenced by traditional English folk music.

> **Tip:** Learn these composers and the names of their pieces.

Sir William Walton (1902-83) wrote a wide range of music, from film scores to opera. He wrote marches for the coronations of King George VI and Queen Elizabeth II but his best-known works are probably *Façade*, which became a ballet, and *Balthazar's Feast*, which is intended to be sung by a large choir.

Benjamin Britten (1913-76) is best known for his operas, which include *Peter Grimes* and *Billy Budd*. He also wrote *A Young Person's Guide to the Orchestra*, which is based on a piece of music by Purcell and introduces the listener to the various different sections of an orchestra. He founded the Aldeburgh festival in Suffolk, which continues to be a popular music event of international importance. 🗩🗩

1) The Proms is a summer season of classical music events. It is organised by the BBC.

2) Frederick Handel wrote the *Water Music* for King George I.

3) Gustav Holst composed *The Planets*.

4) Sir Edward Elgar is best known for the *Pomp and Circumstance Marches*. *March No 1* (*Land of Hope and Glory*) is played at the Last Night of the Proms.

The Last Night of the Proms is held at the Royal Albert Hall in London

🙸🙸 Other types of popular music, including folk music, jazz, pop and rock music, have flourished in Britain since the 20th century. Britain has had an impact on popular music around the world, due to the wide use of the English language, the UK's cultural links with many countries, and British capacity for invention and innovation.

Since the 1960s, British pop music has made one of the most important cultural contributions to life in the UK. Bands including The Beatles and The Rolling Stones continue to have an influence on music both here and abroad. British pop music has continued to innovate — for example, the Punk movement of the late 1970s, and the trend towards boy and girl bands in the 1990s.

There are many large venues that host music events throughout the year, such as: Wembley Stadium; The O2 in Greenwich, south-east London; and the Scottish Exhibition and Conference Centre (SECC) in Glasgow.

Festival season takes place across the UK every summer, with major events in various locations. Famous festivals include Glastonbury, the Isle of Wight Festival and the V Festival. Many bands and solo artists, both well-known and up-and-coming, perform at these events.

The National Eisteddfod of Wales is an annual cultural festival which includes music, dance, art and original performances largely in Welsh. It includes a number of important competitions for Welsh poetry.

The Mercury Music Prize is awarded each September for the best album from the UK and Ireland. The Brit Awards is an annual event that gives awards in a range of categories, such as best British group and best British solo artist. **99**

1) British pop music has had a worldwide impact.
2) Bands from the 1960s, such as The Beatles and The Rolling Stones, still influence pop music today.
3) Music events are held at large venues such as The O2 and Wembley Stadium in London, and the Scottish Exhibition and Conference Centre (SECC) in Glasgow.
4) There are many famous music festivals during the summer, for example Glastonbury, the Isle of Wight Festival and the V Festival.
5) The National Eisteddfod of Wales is an annual cultural festival.
6) The Mercury Music Prize and the Brit Awards recognise achievements by British musicians.

Theatre

66 There are theatres in most towns and cities throughout the UK, ranging from the large to the small. They are an important part of local communities and often show both professional and amateur productions. London's West End, also known as 'Theatreland', is particularly well known. *The Mousetrap*, a murder-mystery play by Dame Agatha Christie, has been running in the West End since 1952 and has had the longest initial run of any show in history.

There is also a strong tradition of musical theatre in the UK. In the 19th century, Gilbert and Sullivan wrote comic operas, often making fun of popular culture and politics. These operas include *HMS Pinafore*, *The Pirates of Penzance* and *The Mikado*. Gilbert and Sullivan's work is still often staged by professional and amateur groups. More recently, Andrew Lloyd Webber has written the music for shows which have been popular throughout the world, including, in collaboration with Tim Rice, *Jesus Christ Superstar* and *Evita*, and also *Cats* and *The Phantom of the Opera*.

One British tradition is the pantomime. Many theatres produce a pantomime at Christmas time. They are based on fairy stories and are light-hearted plays with music and comedy, enjoyed by family audiences. One of the traditional characters is the Dame, a woman played by a man. There is often also a pantomime horse or cow played by two actors in the same costume.

The Edinburgh Festival takes place in Edinburgh, Scotland, every summer. It is a series of different arts and cultural festivals, with the biggest and most well-known being the Edinburgh Festival Fringe ('the Fringe'). The Fringe is a showcase of mainly theatre and comedy performances. It often shows experimental work.

The Laurence Olivier Awards take place annually at different venues in London. There are a variety of categories, including best director, best actor and best actress. The awards are named after the British actor Sir Laurence Olivier, later Lord Olivier, who was best known for his roles in various Shakespeare plays. **99**

1) London's West End ('Theatreland') is well-known for its theatres.

2) Gilbert and Sullivan wrote comic operas such as *HMS Pinafore* in the 19th century.

3) Pantomimes are light-hearted plays based on fairy stories. They are usually performed at Christmas time.

4) Each year, Edinburgh hosts the Edinburgh Festival — a mixture of arts and cultural festivals.

5) The Laurence Olivier Awards includes prizes for best director, best actor and best actress.

The Edinburgh Festival Fringe presents theatrical and comedy performances as part of the Edinburgh Festival

Art

66 During the Middle Ages, most art had a religious theme, particularly wall paintings in churches and illustrations in religious books. Much of this was lost after the Protestant Reformation but wealthy families began to collect other paintings and sculptures. Many of the painters working in Britain in the 16th and 17th centuries were from abroad — for example, Hans Holbein and Sir Anthony Van Dyck. British artists, particularly those painting portraits and landscapes, became well known from the 18th century onwards.

Tip: For more about the Protestant Reformation, see page 23.

Works by British and international artists are displayed in galleries across the UK. Some of the most well-known galleries are The National Gallery, Tate Britain and Tate Modern in London, the National Museum in Cardiff, and the National Gallery of Scotland in Edinburgh.

Notable British artists

Thomas Gainsborough (1727-88) was a portrait painter who often painted people in country or garden scenery.

David Allan (1744-96) was a Scottish painter who was best known for painting portraits. One of his most famous works is called *The Origin of Painting*.

Joseph Turner (1775-1851) was an influential landscape painter in a modern style. He is considered the artist who raised the profile of landscape painting.

John Constable (1776-1837) was a landscape painter most famous for his works of Dedham Vale on the Suffolk-Essex border in the east of England.

The Pre-Raphaelites were an important group of artists in the second half of the 19th century. They painted detailed pictures on religious or literary themes in bright colours. The group included Holman Hunt, Dante Gabriel Rossetti and Sir John Millais.

Sir John Lavery (1856-1941) was a very successful Northern Irish portrait painter. His work included painting the Royal Family.

Henry Moore (1898-1986) was an English sculptor and artist. He is best known for his large bronze abstract sculptures.

John Petts (1914-91) was a Welsh artist, best known for his engravings and stained glass.

Lucian Freud (1922-2011) was a German-born British artist. He is best known for his portraits.

David Hockney (1937-) was an important contributor to the 'pop art' movement of the 1960s and continues to be influential today.

The Turner Prize was established in 1984 and celebrates contemporary art. It was named after Joseph Turner. Four works are shortlisted every year and shown at Tate Britain before the winner is announced. The Turner Prize is recognised as one of the most prestigious visual art awards in Europe. Previous winners include Damien Hirst and Richard Wright. 🙶

1) During the Middle Ages most British art had a religious theme.

2) In the 16th and 17th centuries many of the painters working in the UK were from abroad, for example, Hans Holbein.

3) The National Gallery, Tate Britain and Tate Modern are well-known galleries in London.

4) Other important galleries include the National Museum in Cardiff and the National Gallery of Scotland in Edinburgh.

5) The Turner Prize is an annual award celebrating modern art. Damien Hirst and Richard Wright are past winners.

The former Bankside Power Station in central London is home to Tate Modern

Architecture

❝ The architectural heritage of the UK is rich and varied. In the Middle Ages, great cathedrals and churches were built, many of which still stand today. Examples are the cathedrals in Durham, Lincoln, Canterbury and Salisbury. The White Tower in the Tower of London is an example of a Norman castle keep, built on the orders of William the Conqueror (see pages 16 and 105).

Gradually, as the countryside became more peaceful and landowners became richer, the houses of the wealthy became more elaborate and great country houses such as Hardwick Hall in Derbyshire were built. British styles of architecture began to evolve.

In the 17th century, Inigo Jones took inspiration from classical architecture to design the Queen's House at Greenwich and the Banqueting House in Whitehall in London. Later in the century, Sir Christopher Wren helped develop a British version of the ornate styles popular in Europe in buildings such as the new St Paul's Cathedral.

In the 18th century, simpler designs became popular. The Scottish architect Robert Adam influenced the development of architecture in the UK, Europe and America. He designed the inside decoration as well as the building itself in great houses such as Dumfries House in Scotland. His ideas influenced architects in cities such as Bath, where the Royal Crescent was built.

In the 19th century, the medieval 'gothic' style became popular again. As cities expanded, many great public buildings were built in this style. The Houses of Parliament and St Pancras Station were built at this time, as were the town halls in cities such as Manchester and Sheffield.

In the 20th century, Sir Edwin Lutyens had an influence throughout the British Empire. He designed New Delhi to be the seat of government in India. After the First World War, he was responsible for many war memorials throughout the world, including the Cenotaph in Whitehall. The Cenotaph is the site of the annual Remembrance Day service attended by the Queen, politicians and foreign ambassadors (see page 78).

Modern British architects including Sir Norman Foster, Lord (Richard) Rogers and Dame Zaha Hadid continue to work on major projects throughout the world as well as within the UK.

Alongside the development of architecture, garden design and landscaping have played an important role in the UK. In the 18th century, Lancelot 'Capability' Brown designed the grounds around country houses so that the landscape appeared to be natural, with grass, trees and lakes. He often said that a place had 'capabilities'. Later, Gertrude Jekyll often worked with Edwin Lutyens to design colourful gardens around the houses he designed. Gardens continue to be an important part of homes in the UK. The annual Chelsea Flower Show showcases garden design from Britain and around the world.

Fashion and design

Britain has produced many great designers, from Thomas Chippendale (who designed furniture in the 18th century) to Clarice Cliff (who designed Art Deco ceramics) to Sir Terence Conran (a 20th-century interior designer). Leading fashion designers of recent years include Mary Quant, Alexander McQueen and Vivienne Westwood. 🙶

1) Many British cathedrals, such as in Lincoln and Durham, were built in the Middle Ages.

2) In the 17th century, architects such as Inigo Jones and Sir Christopher Wren designed important buildings. For example, Wren designed St Paul's Cathedral in an ornate style.

3) More simple architecture became popular in the 18th century.

4) In the 19th century, many buildings were built in the medieval 'gothic' style. The Houses of Parliament are an example of this.

5) Sir Edwin Lutyens designed the Cenotaph in Whitehall.

6) Modern British architects, such as Sir Norman Foster and Dame Zaha Hadid work on major projects worldwide.

7) Garden design is also important in the UK — Lancelot 'Capability' Brown designed natural-looking gardens in the 18th century.

8) The Chelsea Flower Show is a famous annual garden show.

9) Modern day fashion designers Mary Quant, Alexander McQueen and Vivienne Westwood are all British.

Literature

❝ The UK has a prestigious literary history and tradition. Several British writers, including the novelist Sir William Golding, the poet Seamus Heaney, and the playwright Harold Pinter, have won the Nobel Prize in Literature. Other authors have become well known in popular fiction. Agatha Christie's detective stories are read all over the world and Ian Fleming's books introduced James Bond. In 2003, *The Lord of the Rings* by JRR Tolkien was voted the country's best-loved novel.

The Man Booker Prize for Fiction is awarded annually for the best fiction novel written by an author from the Commonwealth, Ireland or Zimbabwe. It has been awarded since 1968. Past winners include Ian McEwan, Hilary Mantel and Julian Barnes.

Tip: For more about the Commonwealth, see page 123.

Notable authors and writers

Jane Austen (1775-1817) was an English novelist. Her books include *Pride and Prejudice* and *Sense and Sensibility*. Her novels are concerned with marriage and family relationships. Many have been made into television programmes or films.

Charles Dickens (1812-70) wrote a number of very famous novels, including *Oliver Twist* and *Great Expectations*. You will hear references in everyday talk to some of the characters in his books, such as Scrooge (a mean person) or Mr Micawber (always hopeful).

Robert Louis Stevenson (1850-94) wrote books which are still read by adults and children today. His most famous books include *Treasure Island, Kidnapped* and *Dr Jekyll and Mr Hyde*.

Thomas Hardy (1840-1928) was an author and poet. His best-known novels focus on rural society and include *Far from the Madding Crowd* and *Jude the Obscure*.

Sir Arthur Conan Doyle (1859-1930) was a Scottish doctor and writer. He was best known for his stories about Sherlock Holmes, who was one of the first fictional detectives.

Evelyn Waugh (1903-66) wrote satirical novels, including *Decline and Fall* and *Scoop*. He is perhaps best known for *Brideshead Revisited*.

Tip: Learn the names of each author and what they wrote.

Sir Kingsley Amis (1922-95) was an English novelist and poet. He wrote more than 20 novels. The most well known is *Lucky Jim*.

Graham Greene (1904-91) wrote novels often influenced by his religious beliefs, including *The Heart of the Matter, The Honorary Consul, Brighton Rock* and *Our Man in Havana*.

J K Rowling (1965-) wrote the Harry Potter series of children's books, which have enjoyed huge international success. She now writes fiction for adults as well.

British poets

British poetry is among the richest in the world. The Anglo-Saxon poem *Beowulf* tells of its hero's battles against monsters and is still translated into modern English. Poems which survive from the Middle Ages include Chaucer's *Canterbury Tales* and a poem called *Sir Gawain and the Green Knight*, about one of the knights at the court of King Arthur.

As well as plays, Shakespeare wrote many sonnets (poems which must be 14 lines long) and some longer poems. As Protestant ideas spread, a number of poets wrote poems inspired by their religious views. One of these was John Milton, who wrote *Paradise Lost*.

Other poets, including William Wordsworth, were inspired by nature. Sir Walter Scott wrote poems inspired by Scotland and the traditional stories and songs from the area on the borders of Scotland and England. He also wrote novels, many of which were set in Scotland.

Poetry was very popular in the 19th century, with poets such as William Blake, John Keats, Lord Byron, Percy Shelley, Alfred Lord Tennyson, and Robert and Elizabeth Browning. Later, many poets — for example, Wilfred Owen and Siegfried Sassoon — were inspired to write about their experiences in the First World War. More recently, popular poets have included Sir Walter de la Mare, John Masefield, Sir John Betjeman and Ted Hughes.

Some of the best-known poets are buried or commemorated in Poet's Corner in Westminster Abbey.

Some famous lines include:

'Oh, to be in England now that April's there

And whoever wakes in England sees, some morning, unaware,

That the lowest boughs and the brushwood sheaf

Round the elm-tree bole are in tiny leaf

While the Chaffinch sings on the orchard bough

In England — Now!'

(Robert Browning, 1812-89 — *Home Thoughts from Abroad*)

'She walks in beauty, like the night

Of cloudless climes and starry skies,

All that's best of dark and bright

Meet in her aspect and her eyes'

(Lord Byron, 1788-1824 — *She Walks in Beauty*)

'I wander'd lonely as a cloud

That floats on high o'er vales and hills

When all at once I saw a crowd,

A host of golden daffodils'

(William Wordsworth, 1770-1850 — *The Daffodils*)

'Tyger! Tyger! Burning bright

In the forests of the night,

What immortal hand or eye

Could frame thy fearful symmetry?'

(William Blake, 1757-1827 — *The Tyger*)

'What passing-bells for these who die as cattle?

Only the monstrous anger of the guns.

Only the stuttering rifles' rapid rattle

Can patter out their hasty orisons.'

(Wilfred Owen, 1893-1918 — *Anthem for Doomed Youth*)

1) British writers such as Sir William Golding, Seamus Heaney and Harold Pinter have won the Nobel Prize in Literature.

2) The Man Booker Prize for Fiction is an annual award given to an author from the Commonwealth, Ireland or Zimbabwe.

3) Poetry **has been important throughout British history, and there are many famous British poets:**

   • Chaucer **wrote** *The Canterbury Tales* **in the** Middle Ages.

   • Shakespeare **wrote many** sonnets.

   • William Wordsworth**'s poetry was inspired by** nature.

   • Sir Walter Scott **was inspired by** Scotland.

   • William Blake, John Keats and Lord Byron are examples of popular poets from the 19th century.

   • Wilfred Owen and Siegfried Sassoon were among many poets who wrote about their experiences in the First World War.

4) Many famous poets are buried or commemorated in Poet's Corner in Westminister Abbey (see page 75).

Leisure

66 People in the UK spend their leisure time in many different ways.

Gardening

A lot of people have gardens at home and will spend their free time looking after them. Some people rent additional land called 'an allotment', where they grow fruit and vegetables. Gardening and flower shows range from major national exhibitions to small local events. Many towns have garden centres selling plants and gardening equipment. There are famous gardens to visit throughout the UK, including Kew Gardens, Sissinghurst and Hidcote in England, Crathes Castle and Inveraray Castle in Scotland, Bodnant Garden in Wales, and Mount Stewart in Northern Ireland.

The countries that make up the UK all have flowers which are particularly associated with them and which are sometimes worn on national saints' days:

England
— the rose

©iStockphoto.com/
in.focus

Northern Ireland
— the shamrock

Scotland
— the thistle

©iStockphoto.com/
Frank Rotthaus

Wales
— the daffodil

Shopping

There are many different places to go shopping in the UK. Most towns and cities have a central shopping area, which is called the town centre. Undercover shopping centres are also common — these might be in town centres or on the outskirts of a town or city. Most shops in the UK are open seven days a week, although trading hours on Sundays and public holidays are generally reduced. Many towns also have markets on one or more days a week, where stallholders sell a variety of goods.

Cooking and food

Many people in the UK enjoy cooking. They often invite each other to their homes for dinner. A wide variety of food is eaten in the UK because of the country's rich cultural heritage and diverse population.

Traditional foods

There are a variety of foods that are traditionally associated with different parts of the UK:

- **England**: Roast beef, which is served with potatoes, vegetables, Yorkshire puddings (batter that is baked in the oven) and other accompaniments. Fish and chips are also popular.

- **Wales**: Welsh cakes — a traditional Welsh snack made from flour, dried fruits and spices, and served either hot or cold.

- **Scotland**: Haggis — a sheep's stomach stuffed with offal, suet, onions and oatmeal.

- **Northern Ireland**: Ulster fry — a fried meal with bacon, eggs, sausage, black pudding, white pudding, tomatoes, mushrooms, soda bread and potato bread.

"

1) Some people rent an allotment to grow fruit and vegetables.

2) Some famous gardens are open to visitors, for example Kew Gardens in England and Bodnant Garden in Wales.

3) Each UK country has a national flower: England has the rose, Scotland has the thistle, Northern Ireland has the shamrock and Wales has the daffodil.

4) Shops in the UK are usually open 7 days a week. Many shops have shorter opening hours on Sundays and public holidays.

5) Roast beef, fish and chips, Welsh cakes, haggis and Ulster fry are all traditional foods from across the UK.

Films

British film industry

66 The UK has had a major influence on modern cinema.

Films were first shown publicly in the UK in 1896 and film screenings very quickly became popular. From the beginning, British film makers became famous for clever special effects and this continues to be an area of British expertise. From the early days of the cinema, British actors have worked in both the UK and USA. Sir Charles (Charlie) Chaplin became famous in silent movies for his tramp character and was one of many British actors to make a career in Hollywood.

British studios flourished in the 1930s. Eminent directors included Sir Alexander Korda and Sir Alfred Hitchcock, who later left for Hollywood and remained an important film director until his death in 1980. During the Second World War, British movies (for example, *In Which We Serve*) played an important part in boosting morale. Later, British directors including Sir David Lean and Ridley Scott found great success both in the UK and internationally.

The 1950s and 1960s were a high point for British comedies, including *Passport to Pimlico*, *The Ladykillers* and, later, the *Carry On* films.

Many of the films now produced in the UK are made by foreign companies, using British expertise. Some of the most commercially successful films of all time, including the two highest-grossing film franchises (Harry Potter and James Bond), have been produced in the UK. Ealing Studios has a claim to being the oldest continuously working film studio facility in the world. Britain continues to be particularly strong in special effects and animation. One example is the work of Nick Park, who has won four Oscars for his animated films, including three for films featuring Wallace and Gromit.

Actors such as Sir Laurence Olivier, David Niven, Sir Rex Harrison and Richard Burton starred in a wide variety of popular films. British actors continue to be popular and continue to win awards throughout the world. Recent British actors to have won Oscars include Colin Firth, Sir Anthony Hopkins, Dame Judi Dench, Kate Winslet and Tilda Swinton.

The annual British Academy Film Awards, hosted by the British Academy of Film and Television Arts (BAFTA), are the British equivalent of the Oscars.

Some famous British films

- *The 39 Steps* (1935), directed by Alfred Hitchcock
- *Brief Encounter* (1945), directed by David Lean
- *The Third Man* (1949), directed by Carol Reed
- *The Belles of St Trinian's* (1954), directed by Frank Launder
- *Lawrence of Arabia* (1962), directed by David Lean
- *Women in Love* (1969), directed by Ken Russell
- *Don't Look Now* (1973), directed by Nicolas Roeg

- *Chariots of Fire* (1981), directed by Hugh Hudson
- *The Killing Fields* (1984), directed by Roland Joffé
- *Four Weddings and a Funeral* (1994), directed by Mike Newell
- *Touching the Void* (2003), directed by Kevin MacDonald.

The Development of British Cinema:

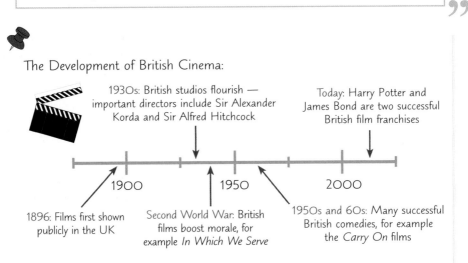

1930s: British studios flourish — important directors include Sir Alexander Korda and Sir Alfred Hitchcock

Today: Harry Potter and James Bond are two successful British film franchises

1900   1950   2000

1896: Films first shown publicly in the UK

Second World War: British films boost morale, for example *In Which We Serve*

1950s and 60s: Many successful British comedies, for example the *Carry On* films

1) Britain is known for its special effects and animation — Nick Park has won four Oscars for his animated films.

2) Famous British actors include Sir Laurence Olivier, David Niven, Sir Rex Harrison and Richard Burton.

3) Many recent British actors have won Oscars — for example, Colin Firth, Sir Anthony Hopkins and Dame Judi Dench.

4) The British Academy of Film and Television Arts (BAFTA) present the annual British Academy Film Awards — the British equivalent of the Oscars.

British comedy

❝ The traditions of comedy and satire, and the ability to laugh at ourselves, are an important part of the UK character.

Medieval kings and rich nobles had jesters who told jokes and made fun of people in the Court. Later, Shakespeare included comic characters in his plays. In the 18th century, political cartoons attacking prominent politicians — and, sometimes, the monarch or other members of the Royal Family — became increasingly popular. In the 19th century, satirical magazines began to be published. The most famous was *Punch*, which was published for the first time in the 1840s. Today, political cartoons continue to be published in newspapers, and magazines such as *Private Eye* continue the tradition of satire.

Comedians were a popular feature of British music hall, a form of variety theatre which was very common until television became the leading form of entertainment in the UK. Some of the people who had performed in the music halls in the 1940s and 1950s, such as Morecambe and Wise, became stars of television.

Television comedy developed its own style. Situation comedies, or sitcoms, which often look at family life and relationships in the workplace, remain popular. Satire has also continued to be important, with shows like *That Was The Week That Was* in the 1960s and *Spitting Image* in the 1980s and 1990s. In 1969, *Monty Python's Flying Circus* introduced a new type of progressive comedy. Stand-up comedy, where a solo comedian talks to a live audience, has become popular again in recent years.

Television and radio

Many different television (TV) channels are available in the UK. Some are free to watch and others require a paid subscription. British television shows a wide variety of programmes. Popular programmes include regular soap operas such as *Coronation Street* and *EastEnders*. In Scotland, some Scotland-specific programmes are shown and there is also a channel with programmes in the Gaelic language. There is a Welsh-language channel in Wales. There are also programmes specific to Northern Ireland and some programmes broadcast in Irish Gaelic.

Everyone in the UK with a TV, computer or other medium which can be used for watching TV must have a television licence. One licence covers all of the equipment in one home, except when people rent different rooms in a shared house and each has a separate tenancy agreement — those people must each buy a separate licence. People over 75 can apply for a free TV licence and blind people can get a 50% discount. You will receive a fine of up to £1,000 if you watch TV but do not have a TV licence.

The money from TV licences is used to pay for the British Broadcasting Corporation (BBC). This is a British public service broadcaster providing television and radio programmes. The BBC is the largest broadcaster in the world. It is the only wholly state-funded media organisation that is independent of government. Other UK channels are primarily funded through advertisements and subscriptions.

There are also many different radio stations in the UK. Some broadcast nationally and others in certain cities or regions. There are radio stations that play certain types of music and some broadcast in regional languages such as Welsh or Gaelic. Like television, BBC radio stations are funded by TV licences and other radio stations are funded through advertisements. 99

1) Comedy and satire are part of British culture.

2) Satirical magazines were first published in the 19th century. *Private Eye* is a satirical magazine published today.

3) Music hall was a type of variety theatre that was popular before television (TV) became widespread.

4) Some music hall stars, such as Morecambe and Wise, went on to perform on TV.

5) Soap operas, such as *EastEnders,* are popular television programmes.

6) Some UK channels broadcast in regional languages. For example, there is a Welsh-language TV channel in Wales.

The satirical magazine *Punch* was created in the 1840s

7) Every home that has a TV or computer to watch TV on must have a TV licence.

8) If you watch TV without a licence, you can be fined up to £1,000.

9) The British Broadcasting Corporation (BBC) is funded by the money from TV licences. Other channels are funded by advertising and subscriptions.

Social networking

66 Social networking websites such as Facebook and Twitter are a popular way for people to stay in touch with friends, organise social events, and share photos, videos and opinions. Many people use social networking on their mobile phones when out and about.

Pubs and night clubs

Public houses (pubs) are an important part of the UK social culture. Many people enjoy meeting friends in the pub. Most communities will have a 'local' pub that is a natural focal point for social activities. Pub quizzes are popular. Pool and darts are traditional pub games. To buy alcohol in a pub or night club you must be 18 or over, but people under that age may be allowed in some pubs with an adult. When they are 16, people can drink wine or beer with a meal in a hotel or restaurant (including eating areas in pubs) as long as they are with someone over 18.

Pubs are usually open during the day from 11.00 am (12 noon on Sundays). Night clubs with dancing and music usually open and close later than pubs. The licensee decides the hours that the pub or night club is open.

Betting and gambling

In the UK, people often enjoy a gamble on sports or other events. There are also casinos in many places. You have to be 18 to go into betting shops or gambling clubs. There is a National Lottery for which draws are made every week. You can enter by buying a ticket or a scratch card. People under 16 are not allowed to participate in the National Lottery.

Pets

A lot of people in the UK have pets such as cats or dogs. They might have them for company or because they enjoy looking after them. It is against the law to treat a pet cruelly or to neglect it. All dogs in public places must wear a collar showing the name and address of the owner. The owner is responsible for keeping the dog under control and for cleaning up after the animal in a public place.

Vaccinations and medical treatment for animals are available from veterinary surgeons (vets). There are charities which may help people who cannot afford to pay a vet. 99

1) You must be aged 18 or over to buy alcohol.
2) Anyone over 16 can drink wine or beer with a meal in a hotel or restaurant, if they are with someone who is over 18.
3) You must be over 18 to go into a betting shop or gambling club.
4) Anyone over 16 can enter the National Lottery.

Places of interest

❝ The UK has a large network of public footpaths in the countryside. There are also many opportunities for mountain biking, mountaineering and hill walking. There are 15 national parks in England, Wales and Scotland. They are areas of protected countryside that everyone can visit, and where people live, work and look after the landscape.

There are many museums in the UK, which range from small community museums to large national and civic collections. Famous landmarks exist in towns, cities and the countryside throughout the UK. Most of them are open to the public to view (generally for a charge).

Many parts of the countryside and places of interest are kept open by the National Trust in England, Wales and Northern Ireland and the National Trust for Scotland. Both are charities that work to preserve important buildings, coastline and countryside in the UK. The National Trust was founded in 1895 by three volunteers. There are now more than 61,000 volunteers helping to keep the organisation running.

UK landmarks

Snowdonia

Snowdonia is a national park in North Wales. It covers an area of 838 square miles (2,170 square kilometres). Its most well-known landmark is Snowdon, which is the highest mountain in Wales.

©iStockphoto.com/Ryan Jones

The Eden Project

The Eden Project is located in Cornwall, in the south west of England. Its biomes, which are like giant greenhouses, house plants from all over the world. The Eden Project is also a charity which runs environmental and social projects internationally.

Edinburgh Castle

The Castle is a dominant feature of the skyline in Edinburgh, Scotland. It has a long history, dating back to the early Middle Ages. It is looked after by Historic Scotland, a Scottish government agency.

Big Ben

Big Ben is the nickname for the great bell of the clock at the Houses of Parliament in London. Many people call the clock Big Ben as well. The clock is over 150 years old and is a popular tourist attraction. The clock tower is named 'Elizabeth Tower' in honour of Queen Elizabeth II's Diamond Jubilee in 2012.

The Giant's Causeway

Located on the north-east coast of Northern Ireland, the Giant's Causeway is a land formation of columns made from volcanic lava. It was formed about 50 million years ago. There are many legends about the Causeway and how it was formed.

©iStockphoto.com/mikeuk

The Lake District

The Lake District is England's largest national park. It covers 885 square miles (2,292 square kilometres). It is famous for its lakes and mountains and is very popular with climbers, walkers and sailors. The biggest stretch of water is Windermere. In 2007, television viewers voted Wastwater as Britain's favourite view.

©iStockphoto.com/DaveBolton

London Eye

The London Eye is situated on the southern bank of the River Thames and is a Ferris wheel that is 443 feet (135 metres) tall. It was originally built as part of the UK's celebration of the new millennium and continues to be an important part of New Year celebrations.

©iStockphoto.com/Mie Ahmt

The Tower of London

The Tower of London was first built by William the Conqueror after he became king in 1066. Tours are given by the Yeoman Warders, also known as Beefeaters, who tell visitors about the building's history. People can also see the Crown Jewels there.

Loch Lomond and the Trossachs National Park

This national park covers 720 square miles (1,865 square kilometres) in the west of Scotland. Loch Lomond is the largest expanse of fresh water in mainland Britain and probably the best-known part of the park.

1) There are many public footpaths in the British countryside.

2) The countryside also offers opportunities for outdoor activities such as mountain biking and mountaineering.

3) In England, Wales and Scotland there are 15 national parks. The countryside in a national park is protected and open to visitors.

4) The National Trust in England, Wales and Northern Ireland and the National Trust for Scotland are charities which take care of important buildings and landscapes in the UK.

5) The National Trust was founded in 1895. Today the Trust has more than 61,000 volunteers.

The UK government, the law and your role

66 The UK is a parliamentary democracy with the monarch as head of state. This section will tell you about the different institutions which make up this democratic system and explain how you can play a part in the democratic process.

The development of British democracy

Democracy is a system of government where the whole adult population gets a say. This might be by direct voting or by choosing representatives to make decisions on their behalf.

At the turn of the 19th century, Britain was not a democracy as we know it today. Although there were elections to select members of Parliament (MPs), only a small group of people could vote. They were men who were over 21 years of age and who owned a certain amount of property.

The franchise (that is, the number of people who had the right to vote) grew over the course of the 19th century and political parties began to involve ordinary men and women as members.

In the 1830s and 1840s, a group called the Chartists campaigned for reform. They wanted six changes:

- for every man to have the vote
- elections every year
- for all regions to be equal in the electoral system
- secret ballots
- for any man to be able to stand as an MP
- for MPs to be paid.

Tip: Make sure you know what the Chartists campaigned for.

At the time, the campaign was generally seen as a failure. However, by 1918 most of these reforms had been adopted. The voting franchise was also extended to women over 30, and then in 1928 to men and women over 21. In 1969, the voting age was reduced to 18 for men and women. 🙿

1) The UK is a parliamentary democracy.

2) In a democracy the whole adult population can vote — either on a particular issue, or to elect someone to make decisions for them.

3) The number of people who had the right to vote increased over the 19th and 20th centuries:

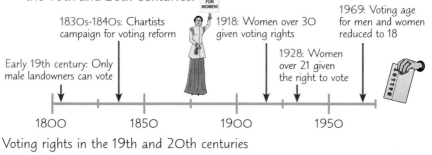

Voting rights in the 19th and 20th centuries

The British constitution

🙶 A constitution is a set of principles by which a country is governed. It includes all of the institutions that are responsible for running the country and how their power is kept in check. The constitution also includes laws and conventions. The British constitution is not written down in any single document, and therefore it is described as 'unwritten'. This is mainly because the UK, unlike America or France, has never had a revolution which led permanently to a totally new system of government. Our most important institutions have developed over hundreds of years. Some people believe that there should be a single document, but others believe an unwritten constitution allows for more flexibility and better government.

Constitutional institutions

In the UK, there are several different parts of government.
The main ones are:

- the monarchy

- Parliament (the House of Commons and the House of Lords)

- the Prime Minister
- the cabinet
- the judiciary (courts)
- the police
- the civil service
- local government.

In addition, there are devolved governments in Scotland, Wales and Northern Ireland that have the power to legislate on certain issues.

The monarchy

Queen Elizabeth II is the head of state of the UK. She is also the monarch or head of state for many countries in the Commonwealth. The UK has a constitutional monarchy. This means that the king or queen does not rule the country but appoints the government, which the people have chosen in a democratic election. The monarch invites the leader of the party with the largest number of MPs, or the leader of a coalition between more than one party, to become the Prime Minister. The monarch has regular meetings with the Prime Minister and can advise, warn and encourage, but the decisions on government policies are made by the Prime Minister and cabinet (see the section on 'The government').

The Queen has reigned since her father's death in 1952, and in 2012 she celebrated her Diamond Jubilee (60 years as queen). She is married to Prince Philip, the Duke of Edinburgh. Her eldest son, Prince Charles (the Prince of Wales), is the heir to the throne.

The Queen has important ceremonial roles, such as the opening of the new parliamentary session each year. On this occasion the Queen makes a speech which summarises the government's policies for the year ahead. All Acts of Parliament are made in her name.

The Queen represents the UK to the rest of the world. She receives foreign ambassadors and high commissioners, entertains visiting heads of state, and makes state visits overseas in support of diplomatic and economic relationships with other countries.

The Queen has an important role in providing stability and continuity. While governments and Prime Ministers change regularly, the Queen continues as head of state. She provides a focus for national identity and pride, which was demonstrated through the celebrations of her Jubilee. 99

1) Queen Elizabeth II is the head of state of the UK.

2) The Queen can advise the Prime Minister, but she does not make decisions on government policy.

3) She has ruled since 1952, and she celebrated her Diamond Jubilee (60 years as monarch) in 2012.

4) She has important ceremonial roles — she opens the new parliamentary session each year.

Queen Elizabeth II is married to Prince Philip, the Duke of Edinburgh

The National Anthem

❝ The National Anthem of the UK is 'God Save the Queen'. It is played at important national occasions and at events attended by the Queen or the Royal Family. The first verse is:

'God save our gracious Queen!

Long live our noble Queen!

God save the Queen!

Send her victorious,

Happy and glorious,

Long to reign over us,

God save the Queen!'

New citizens swear or affirm loyalty to the Queen as part of the citizenship ceremony.

Oath of allegiance

I (name) swear by Almighty God that on becoming a British citizen, I will be faithful and bear true allegiance to Her Majesty Queen Elizabeth the Second, her Heirs and Successors, according to law.

Affirmation of allegiance

I (name) do solemnly, sincerely and truly declare and affirm that on becoming a British citizen, I will be faithful and bear true allegiance to Her Majesty Queen Elizabeth the Second, her Heirs and Successors, according to law.

System of government

The system of government in the UK is a parliamentary democracy. The UK is divided into parliamentary constituencies. Voters in each constituency elect their member of Parliament (MP) in a General Election. All of the elected MPs form the House of Commons. Most MPs belong to a political party, and the party with the majority of MPs forms the government. If one party does not get a majority, two parties can join together to form a coalition.

The House of Commons

The House of Commons is regarded as the more important of the two chambers in Parliament because its members are democratically elected. The Prime Minister and almost all the members of the cabinet are members of the House of Commons (MPs). Each MP represents a parliamentary constituency, which is a small area of the country. MPs have a number of different responsibilities. They:

- represent everyone in their constituency
- help to create new laws
- scrutinise and comment on what the government is doing
- debate important national issues.

The House of Lords

Members of the House of Lords, known as peers, are not elected by the people and do not represent a constituency. The role and membership of the House of Lords has changed over the last 50 years.

Until 1958, all peers were:

- 'hereditary', which means they inherited their title, or
- senior judges, or
- bishops of the Church of England.

Since 1958, the Prime Minister has had the power to nominate peers just for their own lifetime. These are called life peers. They have usually had an important career in politics, business, law or another profession. Life peers are appointed by the monarch on the advice of the Prime Minister. They also include people nominated by the leaders of the other main political parties or by an independent Appointments Commission for non-party peers.

Since 1999, hereditary peers have lost the automatic right to attend the House of Lords. They now elect a few of their number to represent them in the House of Lords.

The House of Lords is normally more independent of the government than the House of Commons. It can suggest amendments or propose new laws, which are then discussed by MPs. The House of Lords checks laws that have been passed by the House of Commons to ensure they are fit for purpose. It also holds the government to account to make sure that it is working in the best interests of the people. There are peers who are specialists in particular areas, and their knowledge is useful in making and checking laws. The House of Commons has powers to overrule the House of Lords, but these are not used often. 🟊🟊

1) The National Anthem of the UK is 'God Save the Queen'.

2) The UK Parliament is made up of two chambers — the House of Commons and the House of Lords.

3) The House of Commons is made up of members of Parliament (MPs) and each MP represents a constituency.

4) MPs are democratically elected by the people living in their constituency and most MPs are part of a political party.

5) The House of Lords is made up of 'peers', who are not elected by the people.

6) Before 1958 many peers were hereditary — seats in the House of Lords were passed down through families. Other peers were either senior judges or Church of England bishops.

7) Since 1958, the Prime Minister has been able to nominate life peers. The leaders of other political parties and an independent Appointments Commission can nominate life peers too.

8) Hereditary peers lost their automatic right to a seat in the House of Lords in 1999.

9) The House of Lords can suggest new laws to be discussed by MPs. It also checks laws passed by the House of Commons.

10) The House of Commons can overrule the House of Lords.

The Speaker

❝ Debates in the House of Commons are chaired by the Speaker. This person is the chief officer of the House of Commons. The Speaker is neutral and does not represent a political party, even though he or she is an MP, represents a constituency and deals with constituents' problems like any other MP. The Speaker is chosen by other MPs in a secret ballot.

The Speaker keeps order during political debates to make sure the rules are followed. This includes making sure the opposition (see the section on 'The government') has a guaranteed amount of time to debate issues which it chooses. The Speaker also represents Parliament on ceremonial occasions.

Elections

UK elections

MPs are elected at a General Election, which is held at least every five years.

If an MP dies or resigns, there will be a fresh election, called a by-election, in his or her constituency.

MPs are elected through a system called 'first past the post'. In each constituency, the candidate who gets the most votes is elected. The government is usually formed by the party that wins the majority of constituencies. If no party wins a majority, two parties may join together to form a coalition.

European parliamentary elections

Elections for the European Parliament are also held every five years. Elected members are called members of the European Parliament (MEPs). Elections to the European Parliament use a system of proportional representation, where seats are allocated to each party in proportion to the total number of votes it has won.

Contacting elected members

All elected members have a duty to serve and represent their constituents. You can get contact details for all your representatives and their parties from your local library and from www.parliament.uk. MPs, Assembly members, members of the Scottish Parliament (MSPs) and MEPs are also listed in *The Phone Book*, published by BT, and in *Yellow Pages*.

You can contact MPs by letter or telephone at their constituency office, or at their office in the House of Commons: The House of Commons, Westminster,

London SW1A 0AA, telephone 020 7729 3000. In addition, many MPs, Assembly members, MSPs and MEPs hold regular local 'surgeries', where constituents can go in person to talk about issues that are of concern to them. These surgeries are often advertised in the local newspaper. 🙶

1) The Speaker has control over debates in the House of Commons. The Speaker is neutral, even though they are an MP themselves.

2) A General Election is held at least every five years in the UK.

3) MPs are elected using the 'first past the post' system — whoever gets the most votes in each constituency becomes the MP.

4) European parliamentary elections are held every five years.

5) They are decided by proportional representation — each party is given seats in proportion to the total number of votes it received.

The government

The Prime Minister

🙶 The Prime Minister (PM) is the leader of the political party in power. He or she appoints the members of the cabinet (see below) and has control over many important public appointments. The official home of the Prime Minister is 10 Downing Street, in central London, near the Houses of Parliament. He or she also has a country house outside London called Chequers.

The Prime Minister can be changed if the MPs in the governing party decide to do so, or if he or she wishes to resign. The Prime Minister usually resigns if his or her party loses a General Election. 🙶

1) The Prime Minister is the leader of the party in government.

2) He or she makes important public appointments.

10 Downing Street, in London — the official home of the Prime Minister

©iStockphoto.com/oversnap

The cabinet

❝ The Prime Minister appoints about 20 senior MPs to become ministers in charge of departments. These include:

- Chancellor of the Exchequer — responsible for the economy
- Home Secretary — responsible for crime, policing and immigration
- Foreign Secretary — responsible for managing relationships with foreign countries
- other ministers (called 'Secretaries of State') responsible for subjects such as education, health and defence.

These ministers form the cabinet, a committee which usually meets weekly and makes important decisions about government policy. Many of these decisions have to be debated or approved by Parliament.

Each department also has a number of other ministers, called Ministers of State and Parliamentary Under-Secretaries of State, who take charge of particular areas of the department's work. ❞

1) The cabinet is made up of about 20 MPs who are chosen by the Prime Minister.
2) Each of these MPs is the head of a government department.
3) The cabinet makes decisions about government policy, but many of these decisions are still debated in the Houses of Parliament.

The opposition

❝ The second-largest party in the House of Commons is called the opposition. The leader of the opposition usually becomes Prime Minister if his or her party wins the next General Election.

The leader of the opposition leads his or her party in pointing out what they see as the government's failures and weaknesses. One important opportunity to do this is at Prime Minister's Questions, which takes place every week while Parliament is sitting. The leader of the opposition also appoints senior opposition MPs to be 'shadow ministers'. They form the shadow cabinet and their role is to challenge the government and put forward alternative policies.

The party system

Anyone aged 18 or over can stand for election as an MP but they are unlikely to win unless they have been nominated to represent one of the major political parties. These are the Conservative Party, the Labour Party, the Liberal Democrats, or one of the parties representing Scottish, Welsh or Northern Irish interests.

There are a few MPs who do not represent any of the main political parties. They are called 'independents' and usually represent an issue important to their constituency.

The main political parties actively look for members of the public to join their debates, contribute to their costs, and help at elections for Parliament or for local government. They have branches in most constituencies and hold policy-making conferences every year.

Pressure and lobby groups are organisations which try to influence government policy. They play an important role in politics. Some are representative organisations such as the CBI (Confederation of British Industry), which represents the views of British business. Others campaign on particular topics, such as the environment (for example, Greenpeace) or human rights (for example, Liberty). 🙶

1) The opposition is the party with the second-largest number of MPs in the House of Commons.

2) Prime Minister's Questions is a weekly event in the House of Commons. It can be used by the leader of the opposition (and any other MPs) to point out the government's failures and weaknesses.

3) The leader of the opposition appoints a shadow cabinet. They challenge the ideas put forward by the government.

4) The three main political parties in the UK are:

| The Conservative Party | The Labour Party | The Liberal Democrats |

5) Some MPs ('independents') are not members of a political party.

6) Pressure and lobby groups (such as the CBI, Greenpeace and Liberty) try to influence government policy.

The civil service

Civil servants support the government in developing and implementing its policies. They also deliver public services. Civil servants are accountable to ministers. They are chosen on merit and are politically neutral — they are not political appointees. People can apply to join the civil service through an application process, like other jobs in the UK. Civil servants are expected to carry out their role with dedication and a commitment to the civil service and its core values. These are: integrity, honesty, objectivity and impartiality (including being politically neutral).

Local government

Towns, cities and rural areas in the UK are governed by democratically elected councils, often called 'local authorities'. Some areas have both district and county councils, which have different functions. Most large towns and cities have a single local authority.

Local authorities provide a range of services in their areas. They are funded by money from central government and by local taxes.

Many local authorities appoint a mayor, who is the ceremonial leader of the council. In some towns, a mayor is elected to be the effective leader of the administration. London has 33 local authorities, with the Greater London Authority and the Mayor of London coordinating policies across the capital. For most local authorities, local elections for councillors are held in May every year. Many candidates stand for council election as members of a political party.

1) Civil servants work for the government, but they are politically neutral.

2) A local authority is a council that governs a local area, e.g. a town.

3) Some areas have two local authorities — a county council and a district council.

4) Large towns and cities usually have one local authority.

5) London has 33 local authorities. However, policy that affects the whole city is decided by the Mayor of London and the Greater London Authority.

6) Local authority councillors are elected in May each year.

Devolved administrations

66 Since 1997, some powers have been devolved from the central government to give people in Wales, Scotland and Northern Ireland more control over matters that directly affect them. There has been a Welsh Assembly and a Scottish Parliament since 1999. There is also a Northern Ireland Assembly, although this has been suspended on a few occasions.

Policy and laws governing defence, foreign affairs, immigration, taxation and social security all remain under central UK government control. However, many other public services, such as education, are controlled by the devolved administrations.

The devolved administrations each have their own civil service. 99

1) Some powers have been taken from the central UK government and given to devolved administrations in Scotland, Wales and Northern Ireland.

2) Central government still controls:
   • defence   • immigration   • social security
   • foreign affairs   • taxation

3) The devolved administrations control other public services, such as education. They each have their own civil service.

The Welsh government

66 The Welsh government and National Assembly for Wales are based in Cardiff, the capital city of Wales. The National Assembly has 60 Assembly members (AMs) and elections are held every four years using a form of proportional representation. Members can speak in either Welsh or English, and all of the Assembly's publications are in both languages.

The Assembly has the power to make laws for Wales in 20 areas, including:

• education and training

• health and social services

• economic development

• housing.

Since 2011, the National Assembly for Wales has been able to pass laws on these topics without the agreement of the UK Parliament.

The Scottish Parliament

The Scottish Parliament was formed in 1999. It sits in Edinburgh, the capital city of Scotland.

There are 129 members of the Scottish Parliament (MSPs), elected by a form of proportional representation. The Scottish Parliament can pass laws for Scotland on all matters which are not specifically reserved to the UK Parliament. The matters on which the Scottish Parliament can legislate include:

- civil and criminal law
- health
- education
- planning
- additional tax-raising powers.

The Northern Ireland Assembly

A Northern Ireland Parliament was established in 1922, when Ireland was divided, but it was abolished in 1972, shortly after the Troubles broke out in 1969 (see page 52).

The Northern Ireland Assembly was established soon after the Belfast Agreement (or Good Friday Agreement) in 1998. There is a power-sharing agreement which distributes ministerial offices amongst the main parties. The Assembly has 108 elected members, known as MLAs (members of the Legislative Assembly). They are elected with a form of proportional representation.

The Northern Ireland Assembly can make decisions on issues such as:

- education
- agriculture
- the environment
- health
- social services.

The UK government has the power to suspend all devolved assemblies. It has used this power several times in Northern Ireland when local political leaders found it difficult to work together. However, the Assembly has been running successfully since 2007. 99

1) The devolved administrations in Wales, Scotland and Northern Ireland each have a slightly different structure and different powers:

	National Assembly for Wales	Scottish Parliament	Northern Ireland Assembly
Location	Cardiff	Edinburgh	Belfast
Members	60 Assembly members (AMs)	129 members of the Scottish Parliament (MSPs)	108 members of the Legislative Assembly (MLAs)
Powers	20 areas, including: education, housing, health, social services and economic development	Anything not reserved for UK Parliament, including: civil and criminal law, health, education, planning and taxes	Areas including: education, agriculture, the environment, health and social services
Notes	Operates in English and Welsh		Power-sharing agreement distributes power between the main parties

2) Northern Ireland first had a parliament in 1922, but it was abolished in 1972 during the Troubles.

3) The Northern Ireland Assembly was set up in 1998, after the signing of the Belfast Agreement (Good Friday Agreement).

The media and government

❝ Proceedings in Parliament are broadcast on television and published in official reports called *Hansard*. Written reports can be found in large libraries and at www.parliament.uk. Most people get information about political issues and events from newspapers (often called 'the press'), television, radio and the internet.

The UK has a free press. This means that what is written in newspapers is free from government control. Some newspaper owners and editors hold strong political opinions and run campaigns to try to influence government policy and public opinion.

By law, radio and television coverage of the political parties must be balanced and so equal time has to be given to rival viewpoints.

Who can vote?

The UK has had a fully democratic voting system since 1928 (see pages 106-107). The present voting age of 18 was set in 1969 and (with a few exceptions) all UK-born and naturalised adult citizens have the right to vote.

Adult citizens of the UK, and citizens of the Commonwealth and the Irish Republic who are resident in the UK, can vote in all public elections. Adult citizens of other EU states who are resident in the UK can vote in all elections except General Elections.

The electoral register

To be able to vote in a parliamentary, local or European election, you must have your name on the electoral register.

If you are eligible to vote, you can register by contacting your local council electoral registration office. This is usually based at your local council (in Scotland it may be based elsewhere). If you don't know which local authority you come under, you can find out by visiting www.aboutmyvote.co.uk and entering your postcode. You can also download voter registration forms in English, Welsh and some other languages.

The electoral register is updated every year in September or October. An electoral registration form is sent to every household and this has to be completed and returned with the names of everyone who is resident in the household and eligible to vote.

In Northern Ireland a different system operates. This is called 'individual registration' and all those entitled to vote must complete their own registration form. Once registered, people stay on the register provided their personal details do not change. For more information see the Electoral Office for Northern Ireland website at www.eoni.org.uk

By law, each local authority has to make its electoral register available for anyone to look at, although this has to be supervised. The register is kept at each local electoral registration office (or council office in England and Wales). It is also possible to see the register at some public buildings such as libraries.

Where to vote

People vote in elections at places called polling stations, or polling places in Scotland. Before the election you will be sent a poll card. This tells you where your polling station or polling place is and when the election will take place. On election day, the polling station or place will be open from 7.00 am until 10.00 pm.

When you arrive at the polling station, the staff will ask for your name and address. In Northern Ireland you will also have to show photographic identification. You will then get your ballot paper, which you take to a polling booth to fill in privately. You should make up your own mind who to vote for. No one has the right to make you vote for a particular candidate. You should follow the instructions on the ballot paper. Once you have completed it, put it in the ballot box.

If it is difficult for you to get to a polling station or polling place, you can register for a postal ballot. Your ballot paper will be sent to your home before the election. You then fill it in and post it back. You can choose to do this when you register to vote.

Standing for office

Most citizens of the UK, the Irish Republic or the Commonwealth aged 18 or over can stand for public office. There are some exceptions, including:

- members of the armed forces
- civil servants
- people found guilty of certain criminal offences.

Members of the House of Lords may not stand for election to the House of Commons but are eligible for all other public offices. 🙾🙾

1) The UK has a free press — what the newspapers say is not controlled by the government.

2) By law though, TV and radio have to give equal time to coverage of different political viewpoints.

3) In the UK, most citizens over the age of 18 can vote.

4) To vote in an election, you have to be on the electoral register. This is updated every September or October, when a registration form is sent to every household.

5) In Northern Ireland anyone entitled to vote must complete their own registration form.

6) Voting takes place at polling stations or polling places. You fill out your ballot paper in private.

7) No one has the right to make you vote for a particular candidate.

POLLING STATION →

Visiting Parliament and the devolved administrations

The UK Parliament

❝ The public can listen to debates in the Palace of Westminster from public galleries in both the House of Commons and the House of Lords.

You can write to your local MP in advance to ask for tickets or you can queue on the day at the public entrance. Entrance is free. Sometimes there are long queues for the House of Commons and people have to wait for at least one or two hours. It is usually easier to get in to the House of Lords.

You can find further information on the UK Parliament website at www.parliament.uk

Northern Ireland Assembly

In Northern Ireland elected members, known as MLAs, meet in the Northern Ireland Assembly at Stormont, in Belfast.

There are two ways to arrange a visit to Stormont. You can either contact the Education Service (details are on the Northern Ireland Assembly website at www.niassembly.gov.uk) or contact an MLA.

Scottish Parliament

In Scotland the elected members, called MSPs, meet in the Scottish Parliament building at Holyrood in Edinburgh (for more information, see www.scottish.parliament.uk).

You can get information, book tickets or arrange tours through visitor services. You can write to them at the Scottish Parliament, Edinburgh, EH99 1SP, telephone 0131 348 5200 or email sp.bookings@scottish.parliament.uk

National Assembly for Wales

In Wales the elected members, known as AMs, meet in the Welsh Assembly in the Senedd in Cardiff Bay (for more information, see www.wales.gov.uk).

The Senedd is an open building. You can book guided tours or seats in the public galleries for the Welsh Assembly. To make a booking, contact the Assembly Booking Service on 0845 010 5500 or email assembly.bookings@wales.gsi.gov.uk ❞

1) The public can listen to UK Parliament debates in the House of Commons and the House of Lords for free. You can write to your MP to ask for tickets or queue on the day.

2) You can also visit any of the devolved administrations:
   - The Northern Ireland Assembly meets at Stormont, Belfast.
   - The Scottish Parliament meets at Holyrood, Edinburgh. The Scottish Parliament building opened in October 2004.
   - The National Assembly for Wales meets at the Welsh Assembly in the Senedd in Cardiff Bay, which opened in March 2006.

The UK and international institutions

The Commonwealth

❝ The Commonwealth is an association of countries that support each other and work together towards shared goals in democracy and development. Most member states were once part of the British Empire, although a few countries which were not have also joined.

The Queen is the ceremonial head of the Commonwealth, which currently has 54 member states (see table below). Membership is voluntary. The Commonwealth has no power over its members, although it can suspend membership. The Commonwealth is based on the core values of democracy, good government and the rule of law.

Commonwealth members		
Antigua and Barbuda	Australia	The Bahamas
Bangladesh	Barbados	Belize
Botswana	Brunei Darussalam	Cameroon
Canada	Cyprus	Dominica
Fiji (currently suspended)	The Gambia	Ghana
Grenada	Guyana	India
Jamaica	Kenya	Kiribati
Lesotho	Malawi	Malaysia

Commonwealth members		
Maldives	Malta	Mauritius
Mozambique	Namibia	Nauru
New Zealand	Nigeria	Pakistan
Papua New Guinea	Rwanda	Samoa
Seychelles	Sierra Leone	Singapore
Solomon Islands	South Africa	Sri Lanka
St Kitts and Nevis	St Lucia	St Vincent and the Grenadines
Swaziland	Tanzania	Tonga
Trinidad and Tobago	Tuvalu	Uganda
UK	Vanuatu	Zambia

The European Union

The European Union (EU), originally called the European Economic Community (EEC), was set up by six western European countries (Belgium, France, Germany, Italy, Luxembourg and the Netherlands) who signed the Treaty of Rome on 25 March 1957. The UK originally decided not to join this group but it became a member in 1973. There are now 27 EU member states (see table below). Croatia will also become a member state in 2013.

EU member states		
Austria	Belgium	Bulgaria
Cyprus	Czech Republic	Denmark
Estonia	Finland	France
Germany	Greece	Hungary
Ireland	Italy	Latvia
Lithuania	Luxembourg	Malta
Netherlands	Poland	Portugal
Romania	Slovakia	Slovenia
Spain	Sweden	UK

EU law is legally binding in the UK and all the other EU member states. European laws are called directives, regulations or framework decisions.

The Council of Europe

The Council of Europe is separate from the EU. It has 47 member countries, including the UK, and is responsible for the protection and promotion of human rights in those countries. It has no power to make laws but draws up conventions and charters, the most well-known of which is the European Convention on Human Rights and Fundamental Freedoms, usually called the European Convention on Human Rights.

The United Nations

The UK is part of the United Nations (UN), an international organisation with more than 190 countries as members.

The UN was set up after the Second World War and aims to prevent war and promote international peace and security. There are 15 members on the UN Security Council, which recommends action when there are international crises and threats to peace. The UK is one of five permanent members of the Security Council.

The North Atlantic Treaty Organization (NATO)

The UK is also a member of NATO. NATO is a group of European and North American countries that have agreed to help each other if they come under attack. It also aims to maintain peace between all of its members. 99

The UK is a member of:

- The Commonwealth — 54 countries who work together with shared goals of democracy and development. The Commonwealth has no powers over its members. The Queen is its ceremonial leader.

- The European Union (EU) — set up in 1957 with the signing of the Treaty of Rome. The UK joined in 1973. It has 27 members (Croatia will join in 2013). EU law applies in all EU countries.

- The Council of Europe — works to protect and promote human rights.

- The United Nations (UN) — set up to prevent war and promote peace and security. It has more than 190 members. The UK is a permanent member of the UN Security Council, which recommends action in times of international crises or conflict.

- NATO — a group of European and North American countries who have agreed to work together to defend each other.

Respecting the law

❝ One of the most important responsibilities of all residents in the UK is to know and obey the law. This section will tell you about the legal system in the UK and some of the laws that may affect you. Britain is proud of being a welcoming country, but all residents, regardless of their background, are expected to comply with the law and to understand that some things which may be allowed in other legal systems are not acceptable in the UK. Those who do not respect the law should not expect to be allowed to become permanent residents in the UK.

The law is relevant to all areas of life in the UK. You should make sure that you are aware of the laws which affect your everyday life, including both your personal and business affairs.

The law in the UK

Every person in the UK receives equal treatment under the law. This means that the law applies in the same way to everyone, no matter who they are or where they are from.

Laws can be divided into criminal law and civil law:

- Criminal law relates to crimes, which are usually investigated by the police or another authority such as a council, and which are punished by the courts.
- Civil law is used to settle disputes between individuals or groups.

Examples of criminal laws are:

- Carrying a weapon: it is a criminal offence to carry a weapon of any kind, even if it is for self-defence. This includes a gun, a knife or anything that is made or adapted to cause injury.
- Drugs: selling or buying drugs such as heroin, cocaine, ecstasy and cannabis is illegal in the UK.
- Racial crime: it is a criminal offence to cause harassment, alarm or distress to someone because of their religion or ethnic origin.
- Selling tobacco: it is illegal to sell tobacco products (for example, cigarettes, cigars, roll-up tobacco) to anyone under the age of 18.

- Smoking in public places: it is against the law to smoke tobacco products in nearly every enclosed public place in the UK. There are signs displayed to tell you where you cannot smoke.

- Buying alcohol: it is a criminal offence to sell alcohol to anyone who is under 18 or to buy alcohol for people who are under the age of 18. (There is one exception: people aged 16 or over can drink alcohol with a meal in a hotel or restaurant — see page 101.)

- Drinking in public: some places have alcohol-free zones where you cannot drink in public. The police can also confiscate alcohol or move young people on from public places. You can be fined or arrested.

This list does not include all crimes. There are many that apply in most countries, such as murder, theft and assault. You can find out more about types of crime in the UK at www.gov.uk

Examples of civil laws are:

- Housing law: this includes disputes between landlords and tenants over issues such as repairs and eviction.

- Consumer rights: an example of this is a dispute about faulty goods or services.

- Employment law: these cases include disputes over wages and cases of unfair dismissal or discrimination in the workplace.

- Debt: people might be taken to court if they owe money to someone.

1) Everyone living in Britain is expected to obey the law.
2) Everyone in the UK is treated equally under the law.
3) UK law is either criminal or civil:

Criminal Law	Civil Law
Laws relating to crimes, usually investigated by the police and punished by the courts. For example, it is against the law to carry a weapon such as a gun or a knife.	Civil law is for settling disputes between people. Employment law is an example of civil law — it is used to settle things such as disputes over unfair dismissal at work.

4) You need to be aware of the laws that affect your everyday life.

The police and their duties

❝ The job of the police in the UK is to:

- protect life and property
- prevent disturbances (also known as keeping the peace)
- prevent and detect crime.

The police are organised into a number of separate police forces headed by Chief Constables. They are independent of the government.

In November 2012, the public elected Police and Crime Commissioners (PCCs) in England and Wales. These are directly elected individuals who are responsible for the delivery of an efficient and effective police force that reflects the needs of their local communities. PCCs set local police priorities and the local policing budget. They also appoint the local Chief Constable.

The police force is a public service that helps and protects everyone, no matter what their background or where they live. Police officers must themselves obey the law. They must not misuse their authority, make a false statement, be rude or abusive, or commit racial discrimination. If police officers are corrupt or misuse their authority they are severely punished.

Police officers are supported by police community support officers (PCSOs). PCSOs have different roles according to the area but usually patrol the streets, work with the public, and support police officers at crime scenes and major events.

Tip: Some members of the police force are volunteers — they are called special constables (see page 143).

All people in the UK are expected to help the police prevent and detect crimes whenever they can. If you are arrested and taken to a police station, a police officer will tell you the reason for your arrest and you will be able to seek legal advice.

If something goes wrong, the police complaints system tries to put it right. Anyone can make a complaint about the police by going to a police station or writing to the Chief Constable of the police force involved. Complaints can also be made to an independent body: the Independent Police Complaints Commission in England and Wales, the Police Complaints Commissioner for Scotland or the Police Ombudsman for Northern Ireland.

Terrorism and extremism

The UK faces a range of terrorist threats. The most serious of these is from Al Qa'ida, its affiliates and like-minded organisations. The UK also faces threats from other kinds of terrorism, such as Northern Ireland-related terrorism.

All terrorist groups try to radicalise and recruit people to their cause. How, where and to what extent they try to do so will vary. Evidence shows that these groups attract very low levels of public support, but people who want to make their home in the UK should be aware of this threat. It is important that all citizens feel safe. This includes feeling safe from all kinds of extremism (vocal or active opposition to fundamental British values), including religious extremism and far right extremism.

If you think someone is trying to persuade you to join an extremist or terrorist cause, you should notify your local police force. 🙶🙶

1) The police protect life and property, prevent disturbances and prevent and detect crime.

2) The police are divided into forces by area, each led by a Chief Constable.

3) In England and Wales, Police and Crime Commissioners (PCCs) are elected by the public. Their responsibilities include:

   • setting local policing priorities

   • setting the budget for their force

   • appointing the Chief Constable.

4) Police officers must obey the law. They are severely punished for any misuse of authority.

©iStockphoto.com/Ann Steer

Police community support officers (PCSOs) work with police officers

5) Al Qa'ida is the most serious terrorist threat to the UK, but there are other threats, e.g. from Northern Ireland-related terrorists.

The role of the courts

The judiciary

66 Judges (who are together called 'the judiciary') are responsible for interpreting the law and ensuring that trials are conducted fairly. The government cannot interfere with this.

Sometimes the actions of the government are claimed to be illegal. If the judges agree, then the government must either change its policies or ask Parliament to change the law. If judges find that a public body is not respecting someone's legal rights, they can order that body to change its practices and/or pay compensation.

Judges also make decisions in disputes between members of the public or organisations. These might be about contracts, property or employment rights or after an accident.

Criminal courts

There are some differences between the court systems in England and Wales, Scotland and Northern Ireland.

Magistrates' and Justice of the Peace Courts

In England, Wales and Northern Ireland, most minor criminal cases are dealt with in a Magistrates' Court. In Scotland, minor criminal offences go to a Justice of the Peace Court.

Magistrates and Justices of the Peace (JPs) are members of the local community. In England, Wales and Scotland they usually work unpaid and do not need legal qualifications. They receive training to do the job and are supported by a legal adviser. Magistrates decide the verdict in each case that comes before them and, if the person is found guilty, the sentence that they are given. In Northern Ireland, cases are heard by a District Judge or Deputy District Judge, who is legally qualified and paid.

Crown Courts and Sheriff Courts

In England, Wales and Northern Ireland, serious offences are tried in front of a judge and a jury in a Crown Court. In Scotland, serious cases are heard in a Sheriff Court with either a sheriff or a sheriff with a jury. The most serious cases in Scotland, such as murder, are heard at a High Court with a judge and jury. A jury is made up of members of the public chosen at random from the local electoral register (see page 120). In England, Wales and Northern Ireland a jury has 12 members, and in Scotland a jury has 15 members. Everyone who is summoned to do jury service must do it unless they are not eligible (for example, because they have a criminal conviction) or they provide a good reason to be excused, such as ill health.

The jury has to listen to the evidence presented at the trial and then decide a verdict of 'guilty' or 'not guilty' based on what they have heard. In Scotland, a third verdict of 'not proven' is also possible. If the jury finds a defendant guilty, the judge decides on the penalty.

Youth Courts

In England, Wales and Northern Ireland, if an accused person is aged 10 to 17, the case is normally heard in a Youth Court in front of up to three specially trained magistrates or a District Judge. The most serious cases will go to the Crown Court. The parents or carers of the young person are expected to attend the hearing. Members of the public are not allowed in Youth Courts, and the name or photographs of the accused young person cannot be published in newspapers or used by the media.

In Scotland a system called the Children's Hearings System is used to deal with children and young people who have committed an offence.

Northern Ireland has a system of youth conferencing to consider how a child should be dealt with when they have committed an offence.

1) The judiciary (judges) interpret the law and make sure trials are fair.

2) The judiciary are independent of the government.

3) The criminal court system is different in different parts of the UK:

	England and Wales	Scotland	Northern Ireland
Minor offences	Magistrates' Court — Magistrates are members of the community and are usually unpaid.	Justice of the Peace Court — Justices of the Peace are members of the community and are usually unpaid.	Magistrates' Court — cases heard by a District Judge (or Deputy) who is a paid legal professional.
Serious offences	Crown Court — a judge and 12-person jury.	Sheriff Court — a sheriff or sheriff and 15-person jury. Very serious cases heard in a High Court.	Crown Court — a judge and 12-person jury.

4) People between the ages of 10 and 17 are tried in Youth Courts.

Civil courts

County Courts

66 County Courts deal with a wide range of civil disputes. These include people trying to get back money that is owed to them, cases involving personal injury, family matters, breaches of contract, and divorce. In Scotland, most of these matters are dealt with in the Sheriff Court. More serious civil cases — for example, when a large amount of compensation is being claimed — are dealt with in the High Court in England, Wales and Northern Ireland. In Scotland, they are dealt with in the Court of Session in Edinburgh.

The small claims procedure

The small claims procedure is an informal way of helping people to settle minor disputes without spending a lot of time and money using a lawyer. This procedure is used for claims of less than £5,000 in England and Wales and £3,000 in Scotland and Northern Ireland. The hearing is held in front of a judge in an ordinary room, and people from both sides of the dispute sit around a table. Small claims can also be issued online through Money Claims Online (www.moneyclaim.gov.uk).

You can get details about the small claims procedure from your local County Court or Sheriff Court. Details of your local court can be found as follows:

- England and Wales: at www.gov.uk
- Scotland: at www.scotcourts.gov.uk
- Northern Ireland: at www.courtsni.gov.uk

Legal advice

Solicitors

Solicitors are trained lawyers who give advice on legal matters, take action for their clients and represent their clients in court.

There are solicitors' offices throughout the UK. It is important to find out which aspects of law a solicitor specialises in and to check that they have the right experience to help you with your case. Many advertise in local newspapers and in *Yellow Pages*. The Citizens Advice Bureau (www.citizensadvice.org.uk) can give you names of local solicitors and which areas of law they specialise in. You can also get this information from the Law Society (www.lawsociety. org.uk) in England and Wales, the Law Society of Scotland (www.lawscot.org.uk)

or the Law Society of Northern Ireland (www.lawsoc-ni.org). Solicitors' charges are usually based on how much time they spend on a case. It is very important to find out at the start how much a case is likely to cost. 🙶

1) How a civil case is dealt with depends on what type of case it is and where in the UK you live:

	England, Wales and Northern Ireland	Scotland
Minor cases, e.g. divorce, personal injury	County Court	Sheriff Court
Serious cases, e.g. involving a large amount of compensation	High Court	Court of Session

2) Small claims can be settled in front of a judge, without a lawyer. A small claim is anything less than £5,000 in England and Wales, and less than £3,000 in Northern Ireland and Scotland.

3) Solicitors are lawyers who:

   • give advice on legal matters

   • take action for clients

   • represent clients in court

4) Solicitors specialise in different areas of law. The Citizens Advice Bureau and the Law Society help people to find the right solicitor.

Fundamental principles

🙶 Britain has a long history of respecting an individual's rights and ensuring essential freedoms. These rights have their roots in Magna Carta, the Habeas Corpus Act and the Bill of Rights of 1689 (see pages 19, 30 and 33), and they have developed over a period of time. British diplomats and lawyers had an important role in drafting the European Convention on Human Rights and Fundamental Freedoms. The UK was one of the first countries to sign the Convention in 1950.

Some of the principles included in the European Convention on Human Rights are:

   • right to life

   • prohibition of torture

- prohibition of slavery and forced labour
- right to liberty and security
- right to a fair trial
- freedom of thought, conscience and religion
- freedom of expression (speech).

The Human Rights Act 1998 incorporated the European Convention on Human Rights into UK law. The government, public bodies and the courts must follow the principles of the Convention.

Equal opportunities

UK laws ensure that people are not treated unfairly in any area of life or work because of their age, disability, sex, pregnancy and maternity, race, religion or belief, sexuality or marital status. If you face problems with discrimination, you can get more information from the Citizens Advice Bureau or from one of the following organisations:

- England and Wales: Equality and Human Rights Commission (www.equalityhumanrights.com)
- Scotland: Equality and Human Rights Commission in Scotland (www.equalityhumanrights.com/scotland/the-commission-in-scotland) and Scottish Human Rights Commission (www.scottishhumanrights.com)
- Northern Ireland: Equality Commission for Northern Ireland (www.equalityni.org)
- Northern Ireland Human Rights Commission (www.nihrc.org). 🙶

1) Respect for an individual's rights and freedoms in UK law originates in Magna Carta, the Habeas Corpus Act and the Bill of Rights (see pages 19, 30 and 33).

2) The UK was involved in drafting the European Convention on Human Rights and Fundamental Freedoms. The UK signed the convention in 1950.

3) Discrimination against someone because of things like their age, sex, race or religion is against UK law.

Domestic violence

❝ In the UK, brutality and violence in the home is a serious crime. Anyone who is violent towards their partner — whether they are a man or a woman, married or living together — can be prosecuted. Any man who forces a woman to have sex, including a woman's husband, can be charged with rape.

It is important for anyone facing domestic violence to get help as soon as possible. A solicitor or the Citizens Advice Bureau can explain the available options. In some areas there are safe places to go and stay in, called refuges or shelters. There are emergency telephone numbers in the helpline section at the front of *Yellow Pages*, including, for women, the number of the nearest women's centre. You can also phone the 24-hour National Domestic Violence Freephone Helpline on 0808 2000 247 at any time, or the police can help you find a safe place to stay.

Female genital mutilation

Female genital mutilation (FGM), also known as cutting or female circumcision, is illegal in the UK. Practising FGM or taking a girl or woman abroad for FGM is a criminal offence.

Forced marriage

A marriage should be entered into with the full and free consent of both people involved. Arranged marriages, where both parties agree to the marriage, are acceptable in the UK.

Forced marriage is where one or both parties do not or cannot give their consent to enter into the partnership. Forcing another person to marry is a criminal offence.

Forced Marriage Protection Orders were introduced in 2008 for England, Wales and Northern Ireland under the Forced Marriage (Civil Protection) Act 2007. Court orders can be obtained to protect a person from being forced into a marriage, or to protect a person in a forced marriage. Similar Protection Orders were introduced in Scotland in November 2011.

A potential victim, or someone acting for them, can apply for an order. Anyone found to have breached an order can be jailed for up to two years for contempt of court. ❞

1) In the UK, anyone (man or woman) who is violent towards their partner can be prosecuted.

2) Any man who forces a woman to have sex with him can be charged with rape.

3) Female genital mutilation (FGM) is illegal in the UK. It is also a criminal offence to take a woman abroad for FGM.

4) Arranged marriages, where both people agree to the marriage, are legal in the UK.

5) Forcing someone to marry is illegal in the UK.

6) A court order can protect someone from being forced into marriage, or protect someone in a forced marriage.

7) Anyone breaking a court order can be put in prison.

Taxation

Income tax

People in the UK have to pay tax on their income, which includes:

- wages from paid employment

- profits from self-employment

- taxable benefits

- pensions

- income from property, savings and dividends.

Money raised from income tax pays for government services such as roads, education, police and the armed forces.

For most people, the right amount of income tax is automatically taken from their income from employment by their employer and paid directly to HM Revenue & Customs (HMRC), the government department that collects taxes. This system is called 'Pay As You Earn' (PAYE). If you are self-employed, you need to pay your own tax through a system called 'self-assessment', which includes completing a tax return. Other people may also need to complete a tax return. If HMRC sends you a tax return, it is important to complete and return the form as soon as you have all the necessary information.

You can find out more about income tax at www.hmrc.gov.uk/incometax. You can get help and advice about taxes and completing tax forms from the HMRC self-assessment helpline, on 0845 300 0627, and the HMRC website at www.hmrc.gov.uk

National Insurance

Almost everybody in the UK who is in paid work, including self-employed people, must pay National Insurance Contributions. The money raised from National Insurance Contributions is used to pay for state benefits and services such as the state retirement pension and the National Health Service (NHS).

Employees have their National Insurance Contributions deducted from their pay by their employer. People who are self-employed need to pay National Insurance Contributions themselves.

Anyone who does not pay enough National Insurance Contributions will not be able to receive certain contributory benefits such as Jobseeker's Allowance or a full state retirement pension. Some workers, such as part-time workers, may not qualify for statutory payments such as maternity pay if they do not earn enough.

Further guidance about National Insurance Contributions is available on HMRC's website at www.hmrc.gov.uk/ni

Getting a National Insurance number

A National Insurance number is a unique personal account number. It makes sure that the National Insurance Contributions and tax you pay are properly recorded against your name. All young people in the UK are sent a National Insurance number just before their 16th birthday.

A non-UK national living in the UK and looking for work, starting work or setting up as self-employed will need a National Insurance number. However, you can start work without one. If you have permission to work in the UK, you will need to telephone the Department for Work and Pensions (DWP) to arrange to get a National Insurance number. You may be required to attend an interview. The DWP will advise you of the appropriate application process and tell you which documents you will need to bring to an interview if one is necessary. You will usually need documents that prove your identity and that you have permission to work in the UK. A National Insurance number does not on its own prove to an employer that you have the right to work in the UK.

You can find out more information about how to apply for a National Insurance number at www.gov.uk "

1) Income tax pays for government services. For example:
   - roads
   - police
   - education
   - armed forces

2) Most people's income tax is automatically taken off their pay by their employer under the 'Pay As You Earn' (PAYE) system.

3) Tax is paid to HM Revenue & Customs (HMRC).

4) Self-employed people pay their tax through 'self-assessment'.

5) Almost everyone working in the UK pays National Insurance Contributions.

6) National Insurance contributions pay for benefits and services such as:
   - the state pension
   - the National Health Service

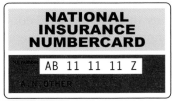

The Department for Work and Pensions issue National Insurance numbers

7) A National Insurance number is a personal account number. It is used to record your tax and National Insurance Contributions.

8) If you have permission to work in the UK you can start work without a National Insurance number, but you will need to get one.

Driving

66 In the UK, you must be at least 17 years old to drive a car or motor cycle and you must have a driving licence to drive on public roads. To get a UK driving licence you must pass a driving test, which tests both your knowledge and your practical skills. You need to be at least 16 years old to ride a moped, and there are other age requirements and special tests for driving large vehicles.

Drivers can use their driving licence until they are 70 years old. After that, the licence is valid for three years at a time.

In Northern Ireland, a newly qualified driver must display an 'R' plate (for restricted driver) for one year after passing the test.

If your driving licence is from a country in the European Union (EU), Iceland, Liechtenstein or Norway, you can drive in the UK for as long as your licence is valid. If you have a licence from any other country, you may use it in the UK for up to 12 months. To continue driving after that, you must get a UK full driving licence.

If you are resident in the UK, your car or motor cycle must be registered at the Driver and Vehicle Licensing Agency (DVLA). You must pay an annual road tax and display the tax disc, which shows that the tax has been paid, on the windscreen. You must also have valid motor insurance. It is a serious criminal offence to drive without insurance. If your vehicle is over three years old, you must take it for a Ministry of Transport (MOT) test every year. It is an offence not to have an MOT certificate if your vehicle is more than three years old. You can find out more about vehicle tax and MOT requirements from www.gov.uk "

1) In the UK, you must be 17 to drive a car or motor cycle, and 16 to ride a moped.

2) Anyone who drives on public roads must have a driving licence.

3) Anyone over 70 must renew their driving licence every 3 years.

4) Newly qualified drivers in Northern Ireland must display an 'R' plate for one year after they pass the driving test.

5) Residents of the UK who own and drive a vehicle must:

   • register their vehicle with the Driver and Vehicle Licensing Agency (DVLA)

   • pay road tax each year and display a tax disc

   • have valid motor insurance

   • take vehicles over 3 years old for an MOT test each year.

A UK road tax disc

Your role in the community

" Becoming a British citizen or settling in the UK brings responsibilities but also opportunities. Everyone has the opportunity to participate in their community. This section looks at some of the responsibilities of being a citizen and gives information about how you can help to make your community a better place to live and work.

Values and responsibilities

Although Britain is one of the world's most diverse societies, there is a set of shared values and responsibilities that everyone can agree with. These values and responsibilities include:

- to obey and respect the law

- to be aware of the rights of others and respect those rights

- to treat others with fairness

- to behave responsibly

- to help and protect your family

> **Tip:** Make sure you learn and understand these values and responsibilities.

- to respect and preserve the environment

- to treat everyone equally, regardless of sex, race, religion, age, disability, class or sexual orientation

- to work to provide for yourself and your family

- to help others

- to vote in local and national government elections.

Taking on these values and responsibilities will make it easier for you to become a full and active citizen.

Being a good neighbour

When you move into a new house or apartment, introduce yourself to the people who live near you. Getting to know your neighbours can help you to become part of the community and make friends. Your neighbours are also a good source of help — for example, they may be willing to feed your pets if you are away, or offer advice on local shops and services.

You can help prevent any problems and conflicts with your neighbours by respecting their privacy and limiting how much noise you make. Also try to keep your garden tidy, and only put your refuse bags and bins on the street or in communal areas if they are due to be collected.

Getting involved in local activities

Volunteering and helping your community are an important part of being a good citizen. They enable you to integrate and get to know people. It helps to make your community a better place if residents support each other. It also helps you to fulfil your duties as a citizen, such as behaving responsibly and helping others. 99

1) British society is based on a set of shared values and responsibilities. For example, obeying the law and helping others.

2) There are some things you can do to be a good neighbour:

- introduce yourself to the people who live near you

- respect your neighbours' privacy

- try not to make too much noise

- keep your garden tidy

- only put your bins out when they are due to be collected.

How you can support your community

66 There are a number of positive ways in which you can support your community and be a good citizen.

Jury service

As well as getting the right to vote, people on the electoral register are randomly selected to serve on a jury. Anyone who is on the electoral register and is aged 18 to 70 can be asked to do this.

Helping in schools

If you have children, there are many ways in which you can help at their schools. Parents can often help in classrooms, by supporting activities or listening to children read.

Many schools organise events to raise money for extra equipment or out-of-school activities. Activities might include book sales, toy sales or bringing food to sell. You might have good ideas of your own for raising money. Sometimes events are organised by parent-teacher associations (PTAs). Volunteering to help with their events or joining the association is a way of doing something good for the school and also making new friends in your local community. You can find out about these opportunities from notices in the school or notes your children bring home.

School governors and school boards

School governors, or members of the school board in Scotland, are people from the local community who wish to make a positive contribution to children's education. They must be aged 18 or over at the date of their election or appointment. There is no upper age limit.

Governors and school boards have an important part to play in raising school standards. They have three key roles:

- setting the strategic direction of the school
- ensuring accountability
- monitoring and evaluating school performance.

You can contact your local school to ask if they need a new governor or school board member. In England, you can also apply online at the School Governors' One-Stop Shop at www.sgoss.org.uk

In England, parents and other community groups can apply to open a free school in their local area. More information about this can be found on the Department for Education website at www.dfe.gov.uk

Supporting political parties

Political parties welcome new members. Joining one is a way to demonstrate your support for certain views and to get involved in the democratic process.

Political parties are particularly busy at election times. Members work hard to persuade people to vote for their candidates — for instance, by handing out leaflets in the street or by knocking on people's doors and asking for their support. This is called 'canvassing'. You don't have to tell a canvasser how you intend to vote if you don't want to.

British citizens can stand for office as a local councillor, a member of Parliament (or the devolved equivalents) or a member of the European Parliament. This is an opportunity to become even more involved in the political life of the UK. You may also be able to stand for office if you are an Irish citizen, an eligible Commonwealth citizen or (except for standing to be an MP) a citizen of another EU country.

You can find out more about joining a political party from the individual party websites. 〟

1) You can be asked to do jury service if you are aged between 18 and 70 and on the electoral register.

2) Parents can help at their child's school by volunteering in classrooms or joining the parent-teacher association (PTA).

3) School governors, or members of the school board in Scotland, are people from the local community.

4) In England, people in a community can apply to open a free school in their local area.

5) British citizens can stand for election as local councillors, members of Parliament or members of the European Parliament.

At election times, members of political parties talk to voters to try to gain support for their party

Helping with local services

   There are opportunities to volunteer with a wide range of local service providers, including local hospitals and youth projects. Services often want to involve local people in decisions about the way in which they work. Universities, housing associations, museums and arts councils may advertise for people to serve as volunteers in their governing bodies.

You can volunteer with the police, and become a special constable or a lay (non-police) representative. You can also apply to become a magistrate. You will often find advertisements for vacancies in your local newspaper or on local radio. You can also find out more about these sorts of roles at www.gov.uk

Blood and organ donation

Donated blood is used by hospitals to help people with a wide range of injuries and illnesses. Giving blood only takes about an hour to do. You can register to give blood at:

• England and North Wales: www.blood.co.uk

• Rest of Wales: www.welsh-blood.org.uk

- Scotland: www.scotblood.co.uk
- Northern Ireland: www.nibts.org

Many people in the UK are waiting for organ transplants. If you register to be an organ donor, it can make it easier for your family to decide whether to donate your organs when you die. You can register to be an organ donor at www.organdonation.nhs.uk. Living people can also donate a kidney.

Other ways to volunteer

Volunteering is working for good causes without payment. There are many benefits to volunteering, such as meeting new people and helping make your community a better place. Some volunteer activities will give you a chance to practise your English or develop work skills that will help you find a job or improve your curriculum vitae (CV). Many people volunteer simply because they want to help other people.

Activities you can do as a volunteer include:

- working with animals — for example, caring for animals at a local rescue shelter
- youth work — for example, volunteering at a youth group
- helping improve the environment — for example, participating in a litter pick-up in the local area
- working with the homeless in, for example, a homelessness shelter
- mentoring — for example, supporting someone who has just come out of prison
- work in health and hospitals — for example, working on an information desk in a hospital
- helping older people at, for example, a residential care home.

There are thousands of active charities and voluntary organisations in the UK. They work to improve the lives of people, animals and the environment in many different ways. They range from the British branches of international organisations, such as the British Red Cross, to small local charities working in particular areas. They include charities working with older people (such as Age UK), with children (for example, the National Society for the Prevention of Cruelty to Children (NSPCC)), and with the homeless (for example, Crisis and Shelter). There are also medical research charities (for example, Cancer Research UK), environmental charities (including the National Trust and

Friends of the Earth) and charities working with animals (such as the People's Dispensary for Sick Animals (PDSA)).

Volunteers are needed to help with their activities and to raise money. The charities often advertise in local newspapers, and most have websites that include information about their opportunities. You can also get information about volunteering for different organisations from www.do-it.org.uk

There are many opportunities for younger people to volunteer and receive accreditation which will help them to develop their skills. These include the National Citizen Service programme, which gives 16- and 17-year-olds the opportunity to enjoy outdoor activities, develop their skills and take part in a community project. You can find out more about these opportunities as follows:

- National Citizen Service: at nationalcitizenservice.direct.gov.uk

- England: at www.vinspired.com

- Wales: at www.gwirvol.org

- Scotland: at www.vds.org.uk

- Northern Ireland: at www.volunteernow.co.uk

1) In the UK, you can register to give blood or donate your organs when you die.

2) Volunteering means working unpaid for a good cause.

3) Volunteering is a way to meet people and make your community a better place to live. It may also help you improve your English or develop new skills.

4) Different UK charities focus on different things:

PDSA — animals   NSPCC — children

The National Trust — the environment

Crisis — the homeless

 Shelter — the homeless   Age UK — the elderly

Cancer Research UK — medical research

Friends of the Earth — the environment

Looking after the environment

 It is important to recycle as much of your waste as you can. Using recycled materials to make new products uses less energy and means that we do not need to extract more raw materials from the earth. It also means that less rubbish is created, so the amount being put into landfill is reduced.

You can learn more about recycling and its benefits at www.recyclenow.com. At this website you can also find out what you can recycle at home and in the local area if you live in England. This information is available for Wales at www.wasteawarenesswales.org.uk, for Scotland at www.recycleforscotland.com and for Northern Ireland from your local authority.

A good way to support your local community is to shop for products locally where you can. This will help businesses and farmers in your area and in Britain. It will also reduce your carbon footprint, because the products you buy will not have had to travel as far.

Walking and using public transport to get around when you can is also a good way to protect the environment. It means that you create less pollution than when you use a car.

1) Recycling is important because:

   - making things from recycled materials uses less energy than making things from new materials

   - it reduces the amount of raw materials we extract from the earth

   - it reduces the amount of rubbish going to landfill.

2) Buying local products reduces your carbon footprint (the amount of greenhouse gases produced as a result of your daily life).

3) Walking and using public transport creates less pollution than using a car. This helps protect the environment.

Important dates in the British calendar

For the test, you need to learn these significant dates in the British calendar.

January

1st New Year's Day

February

14th Valentine's Day

March

1st St David's Day

17th St Patrick's Day

April

1st April Fool's Day

14th Vaisakhi/Baisakhi

23rd St George's Day

October

31st Halloween

November

5th Bonfire Night

11th Remembrance Day

30th St Andrew's Day

December

24th Christmas Eve

25th Christmas Day

26th Boxing Day

31st New Year's Eve/
Hogmanay

Some religious festivals do not have fixed dates, but you still need to know when they happen: Easter is in March or April, Diwali normally falls in October or November, and Hannukah is in November or December.

Other dates to remember are Mothering Sunday (Mother's Day), which is on the Sunday three weeks before Easter, and Father's Day, which is on the third Sunday in June. Eid al-Fitr and Eid ul Adha are two Islamic festivals that do not have fixed dates, but you still need to learn about them (see page 77).

Key dates in British history

Here are some of the most important dates you need to know for the test. There are more dates throughout the book which you should learn too.

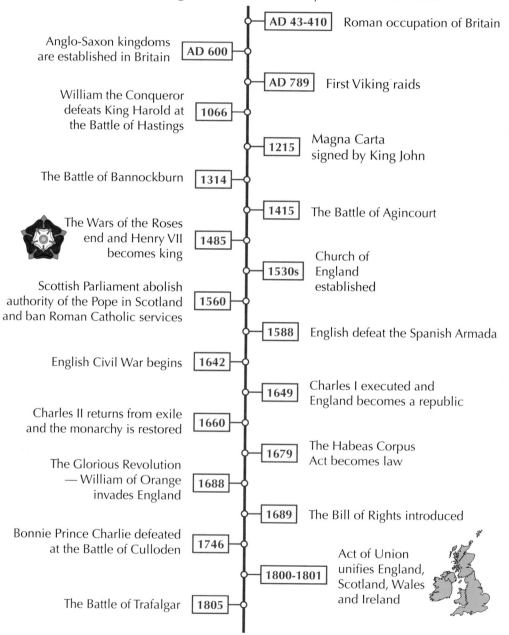

	AD 43-410 Roman occupation of Britain
Anglo-Saxon kingdoms are established in Britain **AD 600**	
	AD 789 First Viking raids
William the Conqueror defeats King Harold at the Battle of Hastings **1066**	
	1215 Magna Carta signed by King John
The Battle of Bannockburn **1314**	
	1415 The Battle of Agincourt
The Wars of the Roses end and Henry VII becomes king **1485**	
	1530s Church of England established
Scottish Parliament abolish authority of the Pope in Scotland and ban Roman Catholic services **1560**	
	1588 English defeat the Spanish Armada
English Civil War begins **1642**	
	1649 Charles I executed and England becomes a republic
Charles II returns from exile and the monarchy is restored **1660**	
	1679 The Habeas Corpus Act becomes law
The Glorious Revolution — William of Orange invades England **1688**	
	1689 The Bill of Rights introduced
Bonnie Prince Charlie defeated at the Battle of Culloden **1746**	
	1800-1801 Act of Union unifies England, Scotland, Wales and Ireland
The Battle of Trafalgar **1805**	

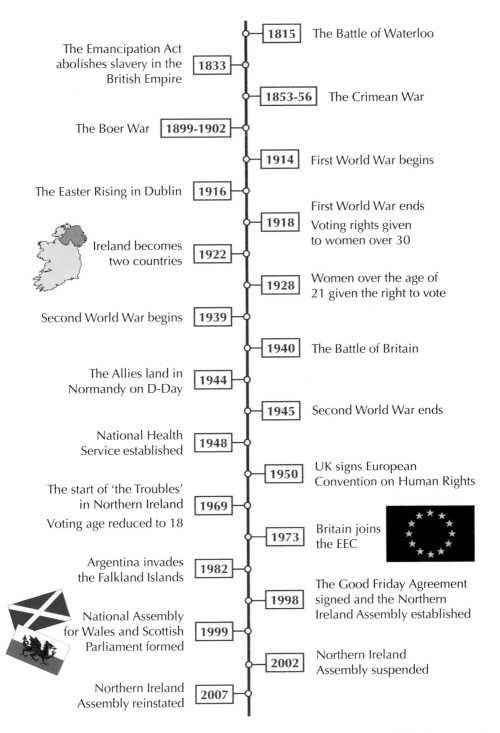

1815	The Battle of Waterloo
1833	The Emancipation Act abolishes slavery in the British Empire
1853-56	The Crimean War
1899-1902	The Boer War
1914	First World War begins
1916	The Easter Rising in Dublin
1918	First World War ends / Voting rights given to women over 30
1922	Ireland becomes two countries
1928	Women over the age of 21 given the right to vote
1939	Second World War begins
1940	The Battle of Britain
1944	The Allies land in Normandy on D-Day
1945	Second World War ends
1948	National Health Service established
1950	UK signs European Convention on Human Rights
1969	The start of 'the Troubles' in Northern Ireland / Voting age reduced to 18
1973	Britain joins the EEC
1982	Argentina invades the Falkland Islands
1998	The Good Friday Agreement signed and the Northern Ireland Assembly established
1999	National Assembly for Wales and Scottish Parliament formed
2002	Northern Ireland Assembly suspended
2007	Northern Ireland Assembly reinstated

Practice Tests

Doing the tests

Once you've learnt the material in this book, doing practice tests is a good way to test your knowledge and prepare yourself for the real test.

There are 20 practice tests in this book. Each practice test contains 24 multiple-choice questions, just like the real thing.

In the test, you will have 45 minutes to answer the questions. Give yourself 45 minutes for each of the practice tests you attempt, so you get used to answering all of the questions within the time limit. The real test will be taken on a computer. For these practice tests, write your answers on a separate piece of paper, or circle the correct answer with a pencil.

Make sure you understand exactly what each question is asking before you choose your answer. Some questions ask for 2 answers — so read the question carefully to avoid making any mistakes. If you are struggling with a question, move on to the next one and come back to it once you've answered all of the other questions. Use any time you have left to check your answers.

When you've finished one of the practice tests, use the answers on pages 211-220 to mark it — in the real test, you need to answer 18 out of 24 questions correctly to pass. There are tips in the answer section to help you with some of the questions you might have got wrong.

For the questions you have got wrong, go back and read the relevant part of the book again. You might find it useful to write your own notes on any bits that you find difficult.

There are more practice questions on the CD-ROM. You can create tests based on the whole of the Home Office text or pick the chapters you want to answer questions on. Using the CD-ROM will help you practise answering questions on a computer, just like in the real Life in the UK test.

Practice Test 1

1. The thistle is the flower that is associated with
   A England
   B Scotland
   C Wales
   D Northern Ireland

2. What is the name of the Stone Age monument in Wiltshire that is a World Heritage Site?
   A Stonehenge
   B Maiden Castle
   C Skara Brae
   D Hadrian's Wall

3. Is the statement below true or false?
   'Each patron saint's day is a public holiday in the UK.'
   A TRUE
   B FALSE

4. Is the statement below true or false?
   'In the late 1970s, imports of goods to Britain were valued at less than the price paid for exports.'
   A TRUE
   B FALSE

5. Is the statement below true or false?
   'The London Eye was built as part of the 2012 Olympic celebrations.'
   A TRUE
   B FALSE

6. Wales became formally united with England by the Act for the Government of Wales during the reign of
   A Henry VII
   B Henry VIII
   C Edward VI
   D Elizabeth I

7. What does MP stand for?
   A Minister of Parliament
   B Man of Parliament
   C Member of Parliament
   D Master of Parliament

8. Mothering Sunday is celebrated on
   A 1 April
   B the Sunday three weeks before Easter
   C 31 October
   D 11 November

9. Which of these statements is correct?

   A Britain has a modern, thriving society.
   B Britain has never been welcoming to migrants.

10. Which TWO of the following are values and responsibilities that are important in British society?

   A To obey the law
   B To help others
   C To teach others
   D To advance your career

11. Which TWO of the following are associated with Sake Dean Mahomet?

   A Opening the first curry house in Britain
   B Introducing 'shampooing' to Britain
   C The campaign against the slave trade
   D Importing tea to Britain

12. Which of these statements is correct?

   A Dame Kelly Holmes won two gold medals for running at the 2004 Olympic Games.
   B Dame Kelly Holmes won two gold medals for running at the 2012 Olympic Games.

13. Which TWO of the following types of plane were used by the Royal Air Force in the Battle of Britain?

   A Concorde
   B Harrier jump jet
   C Spitfire
   D Hurricane

14. Which of the following actions will help reduce your impact on the environment?

   A Buying food from supermarkets
   B Going on foreign holidays
   C Visiting national parks
   D Using public transport rather than driving

15. Is the statement below true or false?
   'William Shakespeare invented many words that are still common today.'

   A TRUE
   B FALSE

16. Is the statement below true or false?
   'In the UK there is a record number of people aged 85 and over.'

   A TRUE
   B FALSE

Practice Test 1

17. Who decides the penalty for a defendant found guilty in a Crown Court?

A The jury
B The judge
C The magistrate
D The prosecutor

18. Which TWO political parties formed a coalition government in May 2010?

A Labour
B Liberal Democrat
C Green
D Conservative

19. How old must you be to drive a car or motorcycle?

A At least 16
B At least 17
C At least 18
D At least 21

20. Which of these statements is correct?

A Supporters of James II were known as Jacobites.
B Supporters of James II were known as Roundheads.

21. Is the statement below true or false?
'The UN Security Council can recommend action when there are international crises or threats to peace.'

A TRUE
B FALSE

22. Glastonbury and the V Festival are summer festivals of

A sailing
B film
C books
D music

23. Which TWO of the following were Christian missionaries from Ireland?

A St Augustine
B St Columba
C St Patrick
D St George

24. Which of these statements is correct?

A Solicitors charges are usually based on whether the client wins or loses the case.
B Solicitors charges are usually based on how much time they have to spend on a case.

Practice Test 2

1. Is the statement below true or false?

   'On average, boys leave school with better qualifications than girls in the UK.'

   A TRUE

   B FALSE

2. Is the statement below true or false?

   'Elections to the Scottish Parliament and the National Assembly for Wales use the 'first past the post' voting system.'

   A TRUE

   B FALSE

3. In which event did Mary Peters win an Olympic gold medal in 1972?

   A Pentathlon

   B 100 metres

   C Rowing

   D Tennis

4. Which TWO of the following are famous British film directors?

   A Ridley Scott

   B David Niven

   C Sir David Lean

   D Sir Edwin Lutyens

5. Is the statement below true or false?

   'During the First World War, Germany, the Austro-Hungarian Empire and the Ottoman Empire were the main Allied Powers.'

   A TRUE

   B FALSE

6. Before 1958, the House of Lords was made up of hereditary peers and which TWO other groups?

   A Senior judges

   B Bishops of the Church of England

   C Roman Catholic bishops

   D Members of the European Parliament

7. Which TWO of the following battles were fought in the Middle Ages?

   A The Battle of Agincourt

   B The Battle of Culloden

   C The Battle of Bannockburn

   D The Battle of the Boyne

8. Which of these statements is correct?

   A Democracy is a system of government where the whole adult population gets a say.

   B Democracy is a system of government where all decisions are made by the Prime Minister.

Practice Test 2

9. The Tate Modern art gallery is housed in the former Bankside Power Station in central

- **A** Cardiff
- **B** Edinburgh
- **C** Belfast
- **D** London

10. Which of these statements is correct?

- **A** The Act of Union, 1800, created the United Kingdom of Great Britain and Ireland.
- **B** The Act of Union in, 1800, created the United Kingdom of Great Britain and Northern Ireland.

11. How old do you have to be to stand for election as an MP in the UK?

- **A** 18
- **B** 16
- **C** 25
- **D** 21

12. Which of these statements is correct?

- **A** The money from TV licences is used to pay for ITV.
- **B** The money from TV licences is used to pay for the BBC (British Broadcasting Corporation).

13. Sir Bernard Lovell built a radio telescope in Cheshire at a site called

- **A** Maiden Castle
- **B** Concorde
- **C** Jodrell Bank
- **D** Housesteads

14. Is the statement below true or false?
'In the 1984 Olympic Games, Jayne Torvill and Christopher Dean won gold medals for synchronised diving.'

- **A** TRUE
- **B** FALSE

15. Which TWO of the following tasks are examples of activities carried out by volunteers?

- **A** Clearing litter
- **B** Working in a pharmacy
- **C** Delivering post
- **D** Helping older people

16. Which of these statements is correct?

- **A** During the 18th century, Britain fought a number of wars with France.
- **B** During the 18th century, Britain fought a number of wars with Italy.

17. Is the statement below true or false?

'In the UK, women cannot be prosecuted for being violent towards their partner.'

  A TRUE

  B FALSE

18. Which of these statements is correct?

  A The Falkland Islands are part of the UK.

  B The Falkland Islands are a British overseas territory.

19. Is the statement below true or false?

'Charles II was succeeded by his brother because his children were too young to inherit the throne.'

  A TRUE

  B FALSE

20. Which people form the judiciary?

  A Magistrates

  B Judges

  C Police

  D Politicians

21. During the reign of Elizabeth I, English settlers first began to colonise

  A north Africa

  B the western coast of Australia

  C the East Indies

  D the eastern coast of America

22. The government department responsible for collecting taxes is

  A HM Treasury

  B HM Revenue and Customs

  C the Department for Business, Innovation and Skills

  D the Department for Work and Pensions

23. Cowes, on the Isle of Wight, is famous for hosting an event in which sport?

  A Sailing

  B Rowing

  C Tennis

  D Motor racing

24. The collection of poems called *'The Canterbury Tales'* was written by

  A William Caxton

  B John Barbour

  C William Shakespeare

  D Geoffrey Chaucer

Practice Test 3

1. Is the statement below true or false?
   'Self-employed people do not need to pay National Insurance Contributions.'

   A TRUE

   B FALSE

2. Which of these statements is correct?

   A The Bayeux Tapestry commemorates the Viking invasion of 789.

   B The Bayeux Tapestry commemorates the Battle of Hastings in 1066.

3. What happens on Bonfire Night?

   A People eat a special meal

   B People give each other gifts

   C People dress up in frightening costumes

   D People set off fireworks

4. Is the statement below true or false?
   'In the 1930s, John Maynard Keynes published influential new theories of philosophy.'

   A TRUE

   B FALSE

5. Which TWO of the following reforms did the Chartists campaign for?

   A For all regions to be equal in the electoral system

   B For women over 21 to have the vote

   C Elections every year

   D For women to be able to stand as MPs

6. Which of these statements is correct?

   A People under 18 are not allowed into betting shops or gambling clubs.

   B People under 21 are not allowed into betting shops or gambling clubs.

7. Which TWO scientists led the team that cloned Dolly the sheep?

   A Sir Ian Wilmot

   B John Macleod

   C Keith Campbell

   D Patrick Steptoe

8. The UK is divided into

   A parliamentary counties

   B parliamentary towns

   C parliamentary constituencies

   D parliamentary coalitions

Practice Test 3

9. Who was the leader of the Labour Party when it was elected in 1997?

   A   Clement Attlee
   B   Tony Blair
   C   Gordon Brown
   D   David Cameron

10. What is the name given to MPs who do not represent any of the main political parties?

   A   Independents
   B   MEPs
   C   Peers
   D   Civil servants

11. Is the statement below true or false?
   'The first professional football clubs in the UK were formed in the late 18th century.'

   A   TRUE
   B   FALSE

12. The railway engine was pioneered by the father and son George and Robert

   A   Stephenson
   B   Nightingale
   C   Brunel
   D   Watt

13. Which of these statements is correct?

   A   School governors are people who want to contribute to children's education.
   B   School governors are senior members of a school's staff.

14. Is the statement below true or false?
   'Emperor Claudius built a wall in the north of England to keep out the Picts.'

   A   TRUE
   B   FALSE

15. Which TWO of the following are Protestant Christian groups?

   A   Baptists
   B   Presbyterians
   C   Roman Catholics
   D   Sikhs

16. Is the statement below true or false?
   'In the 1940s parliament passed new laws giving women the right to equal pay.'

   A   TRUE
   B   FALSE

Practice Test 3

17. Which TWO of the following cities are capital cities of UK countries?

- **A** Belfast
- **B** Manchester
- **C** Newport
- **D** Cardiff

18. Where can you vote in an election?

- **A** Your local council offices
- **B** A polling station
- **C** On your local council's website
- **D** The Electoral Office

19. Is the statement below true or false?
'London's East End is often known as 'Theatreland'.'

- **A** TRUE
- **B** FALSE

20. Which sailor and explorer mapped the coast of Australia?

- **A** William Wilberforce
- **B** Sir Francis Drake
- **C** Captain James Cook
- **D** Admiral Nelson

21. How many people sit on a jury in Scotland?

- **A** 12
- **B** 15
- **C** 16
- **D** 18

22. Which of these statements is correct?

- **A** British citizens are expected to look after everyone in the community around them.
- **B** British citizens are expected to look after themselves and their family.

23. Which of these statements is correct?

- **A** People worried that James II wanted to make England a Puritan country.
- **B** People worried that James II wanted to make England a Catholic country.

24. Which of these statements is correct?

- **A** Anyone can make a complaint about the police by going to a police station.
- **B** Complaints about the police are only handled by the Independent Police Complaints Commission.

Practice Test 4

1. Which of these statements is correct?

   A An important principle of the Enlightenment was that everyone should have the right to their own political and religious beliefs.

   B An important principle of the Enlightenment was that the state should be able to dictate people's political and religious beliefs.

2. Which TWO are examples of criminal offences?

   A Selling tobacco to someone aged 18 or over

   B Carrying a weapon

   C Selling or buying cannabis

   D Selling alcohol to someone aged 18 or over

3. What discount can a blind person claim on a TV licence?

   A 25%

   B 40%

   C 50%

   D 75%

4. Which of these statements is correct?

   A During the Middle Ages, English wool became an important export.

   B During the Middle Ages, English cotton became an important export.

5. Which of the following women was NOT a wife of Henry VIII?

   A Anne of Cleves

   B Catherine of Aragon

   C Jane Seymour

   D Mary Stuart

6. Which of these statements is correct?

   A In British society, intolerance and extremism are only acceptable in certain situations.

   B In British society, intolerance and extremism are not acceptable.

7. The bombing of London and other British cities at night by the German air force was known as

   A The Massacre

   B The Battle of Britain

   C The Blitz

   D The Campaign

Practice Test 4

8. In England and Wales, minor criminal cases are dealt with in a

   A Justice of the Peace Court
   B Sheriff Court
   C Magistrates' Court
   D Crown Court

9. Which TWO of the following British actors have recently won Oscars?

   A Tilda Swinton
   B Charlie Chaplin
   C Dame Judi Dench
   D Richard Burton

10. Is the statement below true or false?
    'Admiral Nelson was in charge of the British fleet at the Battle of Waterloo in 1815.'

    A TRUE
    B FALSE

11. Which TWO of the following did Benjamin Britten write?

    A The Mousetrap
    B Peter Grimes
    C Billy Budd
    D Phantom of the Opera

12. The First World War was fought between

    A 1899 and 1902
    B 1905 and 1907
    C 1914 and 1918
    D 1939 and 1945

13. Is the statement below true or false?
    'In 2012, the cyclist Bradley Wiggins became the first Briton to win the Giro d'Italia.'

    A TRUE
    B FALSE

14. Elizabeth I died childless in 1603 and was succeeded by her cousin

    A James V of Scotland
    B James VI of Scotland
    C James VI of Ireland
    D James VI of Wales

15. Which of these statements is correct?

    A Civil cases are never dealt with in the High Court.
    B Some civil cases are dealt with in the High Court.

16. Which of these cities is NOT in England?

    A Manchester
    B Leeds
    C Birmingham
    D Edinburgh

Practice Test 4

17. Which of these statements is correct?

  A Parents are not allowed to help at their child's school.

  B Parents often help in the classroom at their child's school.

18. The Iron Age hill fort of Maiden Castle is in which English county?

  A Dorset

  B Wiltshire

  C London

  D Yorkshire

19. Is the statement below true or false?
'Using recycled materials to make new products means the amount of rubbish being put into landfill is increased'.

  A TRUE

  B FALSE

20. Is the statement below true or false?
'The Archbishop of Canterbury can only be selected by the monarch.'

  A TRUE

  B FALSE

21. Which TWO of the following organisations can help victims of domestic abuse?

  A The police

  B HM Revenue and Customs

  C The Equality and Human Rights Commission

  D The Citizens Advice Bureau

22. Is the statement below true or false?
'Police officers do not have to obey the law themselves.'

  A TRUE

  B FALSE

23. Is the statement below true or false?
'The Domesday Book contains a list of all the people who lived in the towns and villages of England just after the Norman Conquest.'

  A TRUE

  B FALSE

24. All Acts of Parliament are made in the name of

  A the Prime Minister

  B the ruling political party

  C the United Kingdom

  D the Queen

Practice Test 5

1. The Appointments Commission nominates

   A the Chancellor of the Exchequer
   B the Speaker
   C hereditary peers
   D non-party peers

2. If you cannot go in person to vote, you can vote by

   A text
   B email
   C phone
   D post

3. Which of these statements is correct?

   A Hans Holbein and Sir Anthony Van Dyck were painters from abroad working in Britain in the 16th and 17th centuries.
   B Hans Holbein and Sir Anthony Van Dyck were British painters of the 16th and 17th centuries.

4. Robert the Bruce defeated the English in 1314 at

   A the Battle of Bannockburn
   B the Battle of the Boyne
   C the Battle of Hastings
   D the Battle of Trafalgar

5. Political parties hold policy-making conferences every

   A year
   B three years
   C five years
   D ten years

6. Which of these statements is correct?

   A In the Middle Ages, the nobility, great landowners and bishops sat in the House of Lords.
   B In the Middle Ages, knights and wealthy people from towns and cities sat in the House of Lords.

7. On the Sunday three weeks before Easter, children

   A play tricks on people
   B send cards or buy gifts for their mothers
   C set off fireworks
   D wear a poppy

8. Clement Attlee, who became Prime Minister in 1945, was an MP (member of Parliament) for which political party?

   A Labour
   B Conservative
   C Liberal Democrat
   D Green

9. Is the statement below true or false?
   'During the 1950s, there was a shortage of jobs in the UK.'

   A TRUE

   B FALSE

10. Who is usually tried in a Youth Court?

    A Young people aged between 5 and 18

    B Young people aged between 10 and 21

    C Young people aged between 5 and 17

    D Young people aged between 10 and 17

11. Is the statement below true or false?
    'The settlements of Scottish and English Protestants in Ulster, during the reign of James I, were known as plantations.'

    A TRUE

    B FALSE

12. Which of these statements is correct?

    A The UN was set up after the First World War.

    B The UN was set up after the Second World War.

13. Which of these statements is correct?

    A 'Rotten boroughs' were constituencies controlled by a single wealthy family.

    B 'Rotten boroughs' were constituencies with hardly any voters.

14. Where in the UK is John O'Groats?

    A Northern Ireland

    B England

    C Scotland

    D Wales

15. In which TWO of the following places were British forces involved in conflicts in the 1990s?

    A Afghanistan

    B North Africa

    C Kuwait

    D The Former Republic of Yugoslavia

16. Is the statement below true or false?
    'The BAFTAs are film and television awards that are the British equivalents of the Oscars.'

    A TRUE

    B FALSE

Practice Test 5

17. Which of these statements is correct?

    A During the 19th century the number of people who had the right to vote increased.

    B During the 19th century the number of people who had the right to vote decreased.

18. Henry VIII's first wife, Catherine of Aragon, was a

    A French princess

    B Scottish princess

    C Dutch princess

    D Spanish princess

19. Is the statement below true or false?
'There are more Muslim people in the UK than Jewish people.'

    A TRUE

    B FALSE

20. Is the statement below true or false?
'The police cannot confiscate alcohol from people in public places.'

    A TRUE

    B FALSE

21. Which TWO of the following are fundamental principles of British life?

    A Practising a religion

    B The rule of law

    C Participation in community life

    D Speaking English

22. Is the statement below true or false?
'Pressure and lobby groups are organisations that try to influence government policy.'

    A TRUE

    B FALSE

23. Which TWO sports originated in England?

    A Skiing

    B Rugby

    C Golf

    D Cricket

24. Oliver Cromwell was known by what title when he was the leader of the English republic?

    A President

    B Prime Minister

    C Lord Chancellor

    D Lord Protector

Practice Test 6

1. Penicillin was discovered in 1928 by
   - A Ernest Rutherford
   - B Alexander Fleming
   - C Howard Florey
   - D Ernst Chain

2. The Laurence Olivier Awards celebrate which area of the arts?
   - A Music
   - B Theatre
   - C Dance
   - D Cinema

3. Is the statement below true or false?
   'The European Union was originally called the Council of Europe (CE).'
   - A TRUE
   - B FALSE

4. Is the statement below true or false?
   'Margaret Thatcher was the longest-serving Prime Minister of the 20th century.'
   - A TRUE
   - B FALSE

5. Where do members of the Northern Ireland Assembly meet?
   - A Cardiff
   - B Edinburgh
   - C Belfast
   - D Londonderry

6. Which TWO of the following people are associated with the Elizabethan period?
   - A William Shakespeare
   - B Geoffrey Chaucer
   - C Florence Nightingale
   - D Sir Francis Drake

7. Which of the following is a British overseas territory?
   - A The Channel Islands
   - B Northern Ireland
   - C St Helena
   - D The Isle of Man

8. Which TWO of the following castles did King Edward I build to maintain his power over Wales in the Middle Ages?
   - A Conwy
   - B Warwick
   - C Edinburgh
   - D Caernarvon

9. Is the statement below true or false?
   'In the 18th century, the medieval 'gothic' style of architecture became popular again.'

   A TRUE
   B FALSE

10. In which year did the Spanish send the Armada (a large fleet of ships) to conquer England and restore Catholicism?

    A 1066
    B 1415
    C 1588
    D 1688

11. How often are elections for the European Parliament held?

    A Every year
    B Every five years
    C Every ten years
    D Every twenty years

12. Is the following statement true or false?
    'Sir Robert Walpole was the first man to be known as Lord Chancellor.'

    A TRUE
    B FALSE

13. Is the statement below true or false?
    'The country's population is unequally distributed over the four parts of the UK.'

    A TRUE
    B FALSE

14. Which of these statements is correct?

    A The language spoken during the Iron Age was part of the Celtic language family.
    B The language spoken during the Iron Age was part of the Germanic language family.

15. Which of these statements is correct?

    A An 'allotment' is a piece of land bought by someone so they can grow fruit and vegetables.
    B An 'allotment' is a piece of land rented by someone so they can grow fruit and vegetables.

16. Which of these statements is correct?

    A Volunteers are paid for the work they do.
    B Volunteers are not paid for their work.

17. What was the name of the first Danish king of what is now England?

A Harold

B Cnut

C Alfred the Great

D Stephen

18. Which TWO of the following are roles of school governors or boards?

A Managing staff in schools

B Organising fundraising events in schools

C Ensuring accountability in schools

D Monitoring and evaluating school performance

19. In Scotland, the small claims procedure is used for settling claims under

A £500

B £1,000

C £3,000

D £10,000

20. Which of these statements is correct?

A Roundheads supported the king during the English Civil War.

B Roundheads supported Parliament during the English Civil War.

21. Which TWO are the responsibilities of the judiciary?

A Interpreting the law

B Making sure trials are conducted fairly

C Deciding who becomes Prime Minister

D Representing the people in their constituencies

22. Which of these statements is correct?

A Many of the best footballers in the world play in the English Premier League.

B Many of the best footballers in the world play in the English Football Conference.

23. Is the statement below true or false?
'The Home Secretary is responsible for the country's economy.'

A TRUE

B FALSE

24. Is the statement below true or false?
'The programmes 'Coronation Street' and 'EastEnders' are examples of television comedies.'

A TRUE

B FALSE

Practice Test 7

1. George I, who became king in 1714, was

   A English
   B Scottish
   C French
   D German

2. Is the statement below true or false?
   'New citizens to the UK must swear or affirm loyalty to the Queen as part of the citizenship ceremony.'

   A TRUE
   B FALSE

3. Which TWO of the following are British actors?

   A J K Rowling
   B Sir Rex Harrison
   C Nick Park
   D Richard Burton

4. By which TWO names is the flag of the union of England, Scotland, Wales and Ireland known?

   A Union Flag
   B Union Jack
   C George Cross
   D Tricolore

5. Windermere and Wastwater are in which English national park?

   A The Peak District
   B The Lake District
   C Snowdonia
   D Loch Lomond and the Trossachs

6. The Chartists campaigned for whose right to vote?

   A The working classes
   B The middle classes
   C Women
   D Prisoners

7. Is the statement below true or false?
   'The House of Commons is regarded as the more important of the two chambers in Parliament.'

   A TRUE
   B FALSE

8. Which of these statements is correct?

   A Sir Christopher Cockerell invented the hovercraft in the 1950s.
   B Sir Christopher Cockerell invented the speedboat in the 1950s.

9. Is the statement below true or false?
   'Skara Brae on Orkney, off the north coast of Scotland, is a prehistoric village.'
   A TRUE
   B FALSE

10. Haggis is traditionally associated with
    A England
    B Wales
    C Scotland
    D Northern Ireland

11. What is canvassing?
    A When a British citizen is elected to the European Parliament
    B When a member of a political party tries to persuade you to support their candidate
    C When a member of a political party stands as an MP
    D When someone chooses not to vote

12. Which TWO of the following are British inventions of the 20th century?
    A Radar
    B The World Wide Web
    C Railway engines
    D The Bessemer process

13. A permanent resident or citizen of the UK should
    A know all the kings and queens of England
    B always use their right to vote
    C treat others with fairness
    D be critical of other people's opinions

14. Is the statement below true or false?
    'Northern Ireland and Scotland have their own bank notes which aren't valid in England.'
    A TRUE
    B FALSE

15. Which of these statements is correct?
    A PCSOs provide support for police officers.
    B PCSOs work separately from police officers to solve crimes.

16. During the reign of Charles I, there was a rebellion in Ireland because Catholics there were afraid of the growing power of the
    A Methodists
    B Puritans
    C Presbyterians
    D Cavaliers

Practice Test 7

17. Which of these statements is correct?

  A The Commonwealth has 54 members.

  B The Commonwealth's Security Council has 15 members.

18. What is a member of the National Assembly for Wales known as?

  A Member of Parliament (MP)

  B Member of the Legislative Assembly (MLA)

  C Assembly Member (AM)

  D Member of the Welsh Parliament (MWP)

19. The modern game of golf can be traced back to 15th century

  A Scotland

  B England

  C Wales

  D Ireland

20. Is the statement below true or false?
'Everyone needs to pay their own tax through a system of self-assessment, which includes completing a tax return.'

  A TRUE

  B FALSE

21. Which of these statements is correct?

  A Due to the threat of attack by Vikings, the people of Scotland united under Kenneth MacAlpin.

  B Due to the threat of attack by Vikings, the people of Wales united under Kenneth MacAlpin.

22. Which of these statements is correct?

  A George Frederick Handel, a German-born composer who became a British citizen, wrote the 'Planets'.

  B George Frederick Handel, a German-born composer who became a British citizen, wrote 'Messiah'.

23. Many local authorities appoint a ceremonial leader called a

  A mayor

  B Member of Parliament (MP)

  C civil servant

  D judge

24. Is the statement below true or false?
'In 1688, important English Protestants asked William of Orange to invade England and proclaim himself king.'

  A TRUE

  B FALSE

Practice Test 8

1. Is the statement below true or false?
   'Civil servants have to be politically neutral.'

   A TRUE
   B FALSE

2. Which TWO industries developed during the depression of the 1930s?

   A Shipbuilding
   B Automobile
   C Aviation
   D Information technology

3. Which TWO of the following do you need to become a permanent resident of the UK?

   A To be able to speak and read English
   B To be married to a British person
   C To have lived in Britain for 10 years
   D To have a good understanding of life in the UK

4. Which TWO of the following are British films?

   A Brief Encounter
   B She Walks in Beauty
   C Anthem for Doomed Youth
   D The 39 Steps

5. Emmeline Pankhurst (1858-1928) was a famous

   A nurse
   B suffragette
   C poet
   D Chartist

6. Which of these statements is correct?

   A The White Tower, in the Tower of London, is an example of a cathedral from the Middle Ages.
   B The White Tower, in the Tower of London, is an example of a Norman castle keep.

7. How many times did Henry VIII marry?

   A Once
   B Three times
   C Five times
   D Six times

8. Which of these statements is correct?

   A The National Assembly for Wales meets in Stormont, in Cardiff Bay.
   B The National Assembly for Wales meets in the Senedd, in Cardiff Bay.

Practice Test 8

9. Is the statement below true or false?

'Although slavery was illegal within Britain itself in the 18th century, Britain was a dominant figure in the slave trade.'

A   TRUE

B   FALSE

10. Cars in the UK must be registered with the

A   police

B   DVLA

C   council

D   HMRC

11. Is the statement below true or false?

'Evelyn Waugh is perhaps best known for his novel 'Brideshead Revisited'.'

A   TRUE

B   FALSE

12. With which sport is Dame Ellen MacArthur associated?

A   Running

B   Swimming

C   Sailing

D   Cricket

13. Is the statement below true or false?

'William the Conqueror defeated Harold at the Battle of Hastings in 1086.'

A   TRUE

B   FALSE

14. Which of the following charities works with older people?

A   NSPCC

B   The Red Cross

C   Shelter

D   Age UK

15. Which TWO of the following are forts on Hadrian's Wall in northern England?

A   Housesteads

B   Maiden Castle

C   Vindolanda

D   Sutton Hoo

16. Is the statement below true or false?

'Magistrates decide the verdict of each case that comes before them, but not the sentence that is given.'

A   TRUE

B   FALSE

17. Which of these statements is correct?

   A The patron saint of England is St David.

   B The patron saint of England is St George.

18. The state retirement pension is funded by

   A pension schemes

   B National Insurance Contributions

   C income tax

   D corporation tax

19. Who was the first English king to take the title 'King of Ireland'?

   A Richard III

   B James I

   C Henry VIII

   D Edward VI

20. Which of these statements is correct?

   A By law, radio and television coverage of the political parties must be balanced.

   B By law, radio and television coverage of the political parties can be biased, but not offensive.

21. Is the statement below true or false?
'2 January is a public holiday in Scotland.'

   A TRUE

   B FALSE

22. What proportion of the population of England died during the Black Death in 1348?

   A One tenth

   B One third

   C Half

   D Three quarters

23. What does PCSO stand for?

   A Police county service officer

   B Police community support officer

   C Police community support official

   D Public community service official

24. Which of these statements is correct?

   A Charles I thought that the king should consult Parliament before taking any action.

   B Charles I thought that the king should be able to act without consulting Parliament.

Practice Test 9

1. What is the title of the National Anthem of the UK?

   A   Jerusalem
   B   God Save the Queen
   C   Land of Hope and Glory
   D   Rule Britannia

2. In which TWO battles did the British fight the forces of Emperor Napoleon?

   A   The Battle of Waterloo
   B   The Battle of Trafalgar
   C   The Battle of Britain
   D   The Battle of the Somme

3. John Petts, an artist best known for his engravings and stained glass, was

   A   Scottish
   B   Welsh
   C   Northern Irish
   D   English

4. Is the statement below true or false?
   'Prince William, the Prince of Wales, is the heir to the throne.'

   A   TRUE
   B   FALSE

5. Which of these statements is correct?

   A   The Blair government tightened political control over Scotland and Wales.
   B   The Blair government introduced a Scottish Parliament and a Welsh Assembly with their own powers to legislate.

6. Who celebrates the festival Vaisakhi (or Baisakhi) on 14 April with parades, dancing and singing?

   A   Sikhs
   B   Christians
   C   Muslims
   D   Hindus

7. Which TWO of the following services can solicitors provide?

   A   Give advice
   B   Represent a client in court
   C   Pay compensation to a client
   D   Sell insurance to a client

8. Which of these statements is correct?

   A   The system of land ownership that was used by the Normans is known as feudalism.
   B   The system of land ownership that was used by the Normans is known as democracy.

Practice Test 9

9. Ellie Simmonds won gold medals in the 2008 and 2012 Paralympic Games in which sport?

   A Gymnastics

   B Running

   C Horse riding

   D Swimming

10. Which TWO of the following people are associated with the Enlightenment?

   A David Hume

   B Alexander Fleming

   C William Caxton

   D James Watt

11. Which of these statements is correct?

   A The UK press is controlled by the government.

   B The UK has a free press.

12. Is the statement below true or false?
   'The Reform Act of 1832 allowed all men over the age of 21 to vote.'

   A TRUE

   B FALSE

13. Which TWO of the following religious groups are Protestant?

   A Quakers

   B Jesuits

   C Eastern Orthodox

   D Methodists

14. Dylan Thomas, the poet and writer whose works include 'Under Milk Wood', was

   A English

   B Irish

   C Scottish

   D Welsh

15. Which of these statements is correct?

   A The Crown Jewels are kept in Edinburgh Castle.

   B The Crown Jewels are kept in the Tower of London.

16. Is the statement below true or false?
   'MEPs are elected using a system called proportional representation.'

   A TRUE

   B FALSE

17. Why did Huguenots come to Britain?

   A To escape religious persecution

   B To find work

   C To escape famine in their home country

   D To escape racist attacks

18. Is the statement below true or false?
'National Insurance Contributions pay for government services such as education and the armed forces.'

   A TRUE

   B FALSE

19. Which of the following cities is the capital of Scotland?

   A Glasgow

   B Inverness

   C Aberdeen

   D Edinburgh

20. Which theatre in London is a modern copy of the theatres that Shakespeare's plays were originally performed in?

   A The Old Vic

   B The Royal Opera House

   C The Globe Theatre

   D The Theatre Royal

21. Is the statement below true or false?
'Crown dependencies have their own government.'

   A TRUE

   B FALSE

22. Is the statement below true or false?
'The Speaker of the House of Commons represents a political party.'

   A TRUE

   B FALSE

23. Is the statement below true or false?
'The first Christian communities began to appear in Britain during the 1st and 2nd centuries AD.'

   A TRUE

   B FALSE

24. A General Election is held at least

   A every 3 years

   B every 4 years

   C every 5 years

   D every 6 years

Practice Test 10

1. Which of these statements is correct?

   A   Charles I tried to impose the King James Bible on the Presbyterian Church in Scotland, which led to serious unrest.

   B   Charles I tried to impose a revised Prayer Book on the Presbyterian Church in Scotland, which led to serious unrest.

2. Which of these statements is correct?

   A   The official home of the Prime Minister is 10 Downing Street, in central London.

   B   The official home of the Prime Minister is 11 Downing Street, in central London.

3. Which TWO are famous British inventors?

   A   R A Butler

   B   Alan Turing

   C   Sir Chris Hoy

   D   Sir Tim Berners-Lee

4. Is the statement below true or false?
   'Everyone in the UK has the legal right to choose their religion.'

   A   TRUE

   B   FALSE

5. Which of these statement is correct?

   A   Richard Arkwright, who improved the carding machine, worked in textiles.

   B   Richard Arkwright, who improved the carding machine, worked in shipbuilding.

6. Which TWO of the following international organisations is the UK a member of?

   A   ASEAN

   B   NATO

   C   OPEC

   D   UN

7. Which of these statements is correct?

   A   During the second half of the 20th century, there was a transition from Empire to Federation.

   B   During the second half of the 20th century, there was a transition from Empire to Commonwealth.

8. In the 18th century, Thomas Chippendale was a designer of

   A   furniture

   B   Art Deco ceramics

   C   interiors

   D   gardens

Practice Test 10

9. Which of the following rights will the UK offer to a permanent resident or citizen?

A   a right to a high salary

B   a right to a fair trial

C   a right to a university education

D   a right to bring your friends into the country

10. Is the statement below true or false?
'The origins of the modern Parliament can be traced to the king's council of advisors during the Middle Ages.'

A   TRUE

B   FALSE

11. Which TWO of the following were written by William Shakespeare?

A   Hamlet

B   Paradise Lost

C   Macbeth

D   Beowulf

12. Where is the Scottish Parliament building?

A   Cardiff

B   Glasgow

C   Aberdeen

D   Edinburgh

13. Henry Purcell, a composer of church music and operas, held which post at Westminster Abbey?

A   Dean

B   Choirmaster

C   Organist

D   Bishop

14. Is the statement below true or false?
'In the Iron Age, some people lived in defended settlements called hill forts.'

A   TRUE

B   FALSE

15. On Shrove Tuesday, people typically eat

A   pancakes

B   chocolate eggs

C   roast turkey

D   fish

16. Which TWO of the following institutions are part of the government?

A   The monarchy

B   The NHS

C   The judiciary

D   The Citizens Advice Bureau

Practice Test 10

17. Which of these statements is correct?

   A   Universities and housing associations sometimes advertise for volunteers.

   B   Under UK law, universities and housing associations are not allowed to take on volunteers.

18. Which track and field event did Jessica Ennis win in the 2012 Olympic Games?

   A   Javelin

   B   200 m

   C   Heptathlon

   D   Discus

19. Is the statement below true or false?
'The European Convention on Human Rights includes commitments to the right to life and the right to a fair trial.'

   A   TRUE

   B   FALSE

20. Which of these statements is correct?

   A   'Social security' ensured that Britain's population would be protected from the 'cradle to the grave'.

   B   'Social security' ensured that Britain's population would only be protected after retirement.

21. The electoral register is updated every year in

   A   January or February

   B   April or May

   C   July or August

   D   September or October

22. Which TWO of the following are associated with the Crimean War?

   A   The Victoria Cross

   B   Florence Nightingale

   C   Emmeline Pankhurst

   D   The Battle of Waterloo

23. Prime Minister's Questions take place

   A   every day

   B   every week

   C   once a month

   D   only during general elections

24. Is the statement below true or false?
'Holman Hunt, Dante Gabriel Rossetti and Sir John Millais were part of an important group of artists known as the Pre-Leonardites.'

   A   TRUE

   B   FALSE

Practice Test 11

1. Is the statement below true or false?
'On April Fool's Day, people send anonymous cards to someone they secretly admire.'

A TRUE

B FALSE

2. From which TWO countries did around 120,000 Jews come to Britain, between 1870 and 1914, to escape persecution?

A India

B Russia

C Poland

D Germany

3. Is the statement below true or false?
'Since 1997, some powers have been devolved from the central government to people in Scotland, Wales and Northern Ireland.'

A TRUE

B FALSE

4. Which of these statements is correct?

A The Glorious Revolution was the rapid development of industry in Britain in the 18th and 19th centuries.

B The Industrial Revolution was the rapid development of industry in Britain in the 18th and 19th centuries.

5. Is the statement below true or false?
'MPs are elected through a system called proportional representation.'

A TRUE

B FALSE

6. The first formal anti-slavery groups, who petitioned Parliament to ban slavery, were set up by

A Quakers

B Huguenots

C Jews

D Catholics

7. Which TWO of the following are notable British writers?

A Ellie Simmonds

B Ken Russell

C Sir Kingsley Amis

D Graham Greene

8. Which of these statements is correct?

A It is the task of judges to make the law.

B It is the task of judges to interpret the law.

Practice Test 11

9. The English republic, known as the Commonwealth, had no

- **A** monarch
- **B** prime minister
- **C** parliament
- **D** official Church

10. Which of these statements is correct?

- **A** Land's End is in the south-west corner of England.
- **B** Land's End is in the north-west corner of Scotland.

11. Is the statement below true or false?
'During the Middle Ages, English kings fought a number of wars abroad.'

- **A** TRUE
- **B** FALSE

12. Which of these statements is correct?

- **A** Sir William Golding, Seamus Heaney and Harold Pinter have won the Nobel Prize in Literature.
- **B** Sir William Golding, Seamus Heaney and Harold Pinter have won the Nobel Prize in Physics.

13. After the Battle of the Boyne, restrictions were placed on

- **A** the Church of Scotland
- **B** the Roman Catholic Church in Ireland
- **C** the Church of England
- **D** the Puritans

14. The Queen has which TWO of the following responsibilities?

- **A** She makes the final decision on government policies
- **B** She represents the UK to the rest of the world
- **C** She opens the new parliamentary session each year
- **D** She chairs debates in Parliament

15. In which sport did Bobby Moore captain England to World Cup victory in 1966?

- **A** Football
- **B** Rugby
- **C** Cricket
- **D** Golf

16. Which TWO of the following matters can the Northern Ireland Assembly make decisions on?

- **A** National defence
- **B** Agriculture
- **C** Social services
- **D** Taxation

Practice Test 11

17. During the Second World War, more than 300,000 men were evacuated from the beaches around

    A   Calais

    B   the Somme

    C   Singapore

    D   Dunkirk

18. By becoming a permanent resident or citizen of the UK you will

    A   give up your own values and beliefs

    B   agree to respect the laws and values of the UK

    C   be obliged to work in the UK

    D   stay in the UK for your lifetime

19. Which of these statements is correct?

    A   The people of the Bronze Age made weapons and tools out of bronze.

    B   The people of the Bronze Age made weapons and tools out of iron.

20. Is the statement below true or false?
'New citizens do not swear or affirm loyalty to the Queen or to any members of the royal family.'

    A   TRUE

    B   FALSE

21. 'The Fringe' is a part of which annual Scottish festival?

    A   The Highland Games

    B   The Edinburgh Festival

    C   Burns Night

    D   The Dundee Festival

22. If you're over 70, how long is your driving licence valid for?

    A   2 years at a time

    B   3 years at a time

    C   5 years at a time

    D   10 years at a time

23. Is the statement below true or false?
'When Henry VII died he was succeeded by his son Richard III.'

    A   TRUE

    B   FALSE

24. Who can be asked to serve on a jury?

    A   Anyone over the age of 18

    B   Anyone on the electoral register

    C   Anyone on the electoral register between the ages of 18 and 70

    D   Anyone on the electoral register between the ages of 18 and 65

Practice Test 12

1. Florence Nightingale (1820-1910) worked as a nurse in Turkey during

   A   the Napoleonic Wars
   B   the Crimean War
   C   the Boer War
   D   the First World War

2. Many parts of the countryside and places of interest are kept open by

   A   Greenpeace
   B   the NHS
   C   the National Trust and the National Trust for Scotland
   D   the National Heritage and the National Heritage for Scotland

3. Which of these statements is correct?

   A   The UK is one of the five permanent members of the UN Security Council.
   B   The UK is one of the fifteen permanent members of the UN Security Council.

4. The trigger for the First World War was the assassination of the Austrian Archduke

   A   Franz Ferdinand
   B   Napoleon
   C   Kaiser Wilhelm
   D   Adolf Hitler

5. Which TWO of the following are important Christian festivals?

   A   Remembrance Day
   B   Christmas
   C   Easter
   D   Halloween

6. Isaac Newton, who studied at Cambridge University, is famous for working on

   A   electricity
   B   penicillin
   C   fossils
   D   gravity

7. Permanent residents and citizens of the UK agree to

   A   speak English at all times
   B   give up their own cultural heritage
   C   accept the responsibilities of being a British citizen
   D   stay in the UK for their lifetime

8. During the Middle Ages, many people in Scotland continued to speak which language?

   A   Anglo-Saxon
   B   Irish
   C   French
   D   Gaelic

9. Is the statement below true or false?

   'It is illegal to buy and sell drugs such as heroin, cocaine, ecstasy and cannabis.'

   A   TRUE

   B   FALSE

10. Which of these statements is correct?

   A   Sir Francis Drake's ship, the 'Golden Hind', was one of the first to circumnavigate (sail right around) the world.

   B   Sir Francis Drake's ship, the 'Golden Hind', was one of the first to circumnavigate (sail right around) Britain.

11. Which TWO of the following are traditional pub games?

   A   Darts

   B   Chess

   C   Pool

   D   Football

12. Which of these statements is correct?

   A   The Harrier jump jet can take off vertically.

   B   The Harrier jump jet can take off backwards.

13. Which of these statements is correct?

   A   The king or queen rules the UK.

   B   The king or queen does not rule the UK, but appoints the government.

14. Is the statement below true or false?

   The novel 'Lucky Jim' was written by the novelist and poet Thomas Hardy.'

   A   TRUE

   B   FALSE

15. Is the statement below true or false?

   'Voluntary work only brings benefits to you and not to your community.'

   A   TRUE

   B   FALSE

16. The Norman Conquest of Britain began when WIlliam, Duke of Normandy, invaded England in

   A   789

   B   1066

   C   1215

   D   1348

17. Is the statement below true or false?

'A hearing in a small claims procedure is held in front of a magistrate in a court.'

A TRUE

B FALSE

18. Is the statement below true or false?

'Protestant ideas gradually gained strength in England, Wales and Ireland during the 14th century.'

A TRUE

B FALSE

19. Is the statement below true or false?

'Since 1999, hereditary peers have gained the automatic right to attend the House of Lords.'

A TRUE

B FALSE

20. In how many consecutive Olympic Games did Sir Steve Redgrave win gold medals in rowing?

A Two

B Three

C Four

D Five

21. In Northern Ireland, you can make a complaint about the police to

A the Police Ombudsman for Northern Ireland

B the Police Commissioner of Northern Ireland

C the Northern Ireland Police Complaints Commission

D the Serious Complaints Office

22. From which TWO areas did Britain import sugar and tobacco?

A North America

B Japan

C The West Indies

D Australia

23. Which of the following is NOT illegal in the UK?

A Female genital mutilation

B Arranged marriage

C Forced marriage

D Domestic violence

24. Which TWO of the following are British garden designers?

A Gertrude Jekyll

B Robert Adam

C Lancelot 'Capability' Brown

D Mary Quant

Practice Test 13

1. Is the statement below true or false?
   'The number of men who study at university in the UK is double the number of women.'

   A TRUE

   B FALSE

2. Is the statement below true or false?
   'Citizens of the UK are not responsible for looking after the area in which they live.'

   A TRUE

   B FALSE

3. Which TWO of the following countries were granted independence from Britain in 1947?

   A Australia

   B India

   C Pakistan

   D South Africa

4. Is the statement below true or false?
   'When the Queen opens a new parliamentary session, she gives a speech summarising her policies for the year ahead.'

   A TRUE

   B FALSE

5. Which TWO of the following were members of the Royal Society?

   A Sir Robert Walpole

   B Sir Isaac Newton

   C Oliver Cromwell

   D Sir Edmund Halley

6. The Church of England is known by which TWO names in other countries?

   A Roman Catholic Church

   B Episcopal Church

   C Anglican Church

   D Presbyterian Church

7. Henry VIII was famous for breaking away from the Church of

   A Rome

   B England

   C Scotland

   D Canterbury

8. Who investigates crimes?

   A The army

   B MPs

   C The police

   D Lawyers

9. Which TWO of the following developed because of the Bessemer process for the mass production of steel?

   A   The shipbuilding industry
   B   The brewing industry
   C   Farming
   D   The railways

10. Is the statement below true or false?
    'The poem 'If' was written by Rudyard Kipling.'

    A   TRUE
    B   FALSE

11. In which decade was the voting age for men and women reduced from 21 to 18?

    A   1920s
    B   1930s
    C   1950s
    D   1960s

12. Is the statement below true or false?
    'The first ATM (cashpoint) was put into use in 1987.'

    A   TRUE
    B   FALSE

13. If you have a driving licence from the United States of America, you can drive in the UK for

    A   as long as your licence is valid
    B   two years
    C   up to 6 months
    D   up to 12 months

14. Where is the city of Swansea?

    A   Scotland
    B   Wales
    C   England
    D   Northern Ireland

15. Which TWO people made penicillin into a usable drug?

    A   Howard Florey
    B   Ernest Rutherford
    C   Aneurin (Nye) Bevan
    D   Ernst Chain

16. Is the statement below true or false?
    'David Hockney was an important contributor to the 'pop art' movement of the 1960s.'

    A   TRUE
    B   FALSE

Practice Test 13

17. Which of these statements is correct?

   A   The National Citizen Service programme gives teenagers the opportunity to enjoy outdoor activities and take part in community projects.

   B   The National Citizen Service programme organises community service for teenagers who have committed crimes.

18. St David's day is on

   A   1 January

   B   1 March

   C   17 March

   D   30 November

19. Which of these statements is correct?

   A   NATO aims to maintain peace between all of its members.

   B   NATO aims to improve trade between the UK and North America.

20. In 1660, Parliament invited Charles II to come back from exile in an event known as

   A   the Enlightenment

   B   the Restoration

   C   the Reformation

   D   the Commonwealth

21. The constitution of the UK

   A   was only written down in recent years

   B   is not written down on one document

   C   was written after a revolution

   D   was first written down in the 17th century

22. Which of these statements is correct?

   A   The 'Carry On' films are British comedies.

   B   The 'Carry On' films are British dramas.

23. Which of these statements is correct?

   A   The Magna Carta confirmed that the king was above the law.

   B   The Magna Carta established the idea that even the king was subject to the law.

24. The Northern Ireland Parliament was abolished in 1972, shortly after the beginning of the

   A   Reformation

   B   Troubles

   C   Glorious Revolution

   D   partition of Ireland

Practice Test 14

1. Which of these statements is correct?

   A MRI (magnetic resonance imaging) allows doctors to obtain invasive images of human internal organs.

   B MRI (magnetic resonance imaging) allows doctors to obtain non-invasive images of human internal organs.

2. Is the statement below true or false?
   'Criminal law is used to settle disputes between individuals or groups.'

   A TRUE
   B FALSE

3. Which of these statements is correct?

   A During the mid 19th century, Ireland suffered a famine when the oat crop failed.

   B During the mid 19th century, Ireland suffered a famine when the potato crop failed.

4. The nickname for the great bell of the clock at the Houses of Parliament in London is

   A The London Eye
   B Giant Ben
   C Big Ben
   D Big Bill

5. The Welsh flag has a green and white background and a red

   A lion
   B bear
   C eagle
   D dragon

6. Which of these statements is correct?

   A Both arranged marriage and forced marriage are illegal in the UK.

   B Although forced marriage is illegal in the UK, arranged marriage is not.

7. Is the statement below true or false?
   'From 1695, newspapers were allowed to operate without a government licence.'

   A TRUE
   B FALSE

8. Is the statement below true or false?
   'The 40 days before Easter are known as Harvest Festival.'

   A TRUE
   B FALSE

9. How are people selected to serve on a jury?

A In alphabetical groups

B At random

C By employment type

D By age

10. Samuel Pepys was famous for writing

A poems

B plays

C letters

D a diary

11. Which of these statements is correct?

A The government is usually formed by the party which wins the majority of votes.

B The government is usually formed by the party which wins the majority of constituencies.

12. Is the statement below true or false?
'During the reigns of Elizabeth I and James I, many people in Ireland opposed rule by the Protestant government in England.'

A TRUE

B FALSE

13. Is the statement below true or false?
'People aged over 65 can apply for a free TV licence.'

A TRUE

B FALSE

14. Which Anglo-Saxon poem tells of its hero's battles against monsters?

A Home Thoughts from Abroad

B The Canterbury Tales

C Beowulf

D The Daffodils

15. Which TWO of the following were agreed in the Magna Carta?

A Limits on the king's power

B Parliament had control over who could be king

C The protection of the rights of the nobility

D No one could be held in prison unlawfully

16. Which TWO of the following are aims of the United Nations?

A To regulate the world's economy

B To prevent war

C To promote international peace and security

D To spread democracy across the world

17. Which of these statements is correct?

    A During the Middle Ages, there was little immigration to England.

    B During the Middle Ages, many skilled workers came to England from abroad.

18. Which of these countries is not part of 'Great Britain'?

    A England

    B Wales

    C Northern Ireland

    D Scotland

19. Is the statement below true or false?
'The House of Lords is normally more independent of the government than the House of Commons.'

    A TRUE

    B FALSE

20. Which king united the Anglo-Saxon kingdoms against the Vikings?

    A Cnut

    B Henry I

    C Alfred the Great

    D Harold

21. Which of these statements is correct?

    A Many theatres produce a pantomime at Easter time.

    B Many theatres produce a pantomime at Christmas time.

22. Which TWO of the following groups of people can vote in a UK General Election?

    A UK-born citizens who are aged over 18

    B Citizens of other EU states who are aged over 18

    C Adult citizens of the Commonwealth who are resident in the UK

    D UK-born citizens who are aged 16 and 17

23. Which TWO universities compete in a yearly rowing race on the river Thames?

    A Durham

    B Warwick

    C Cambridge

    D Oxford

24. If your car is over three years old, how often must you take it for an MOT test?

    A Every year

    B Every two years

    C Every three years

    D Every five years

Practice Test 15

1. Which of these statements is correct?

    A You can contact your MP at their office in the House of Commons.

    B You can contact your MP at their office in the House of Lords.

2. Is the statement below true or false?
   'The spiritual leader of the Church of England is the Archbishop of Canterbury.'

    A TRUE

    B FALSE

3. Which of these statements is correct?

    A The UK joined the European Economic Community (EEC) in 1957.

    B The UK joined the European Economic Community (EEC) in 1973.

4. Which of these statements is correct?

    A Judges are only involved in criminal court cases.

    B Judges make decisions in disputes between members of the public or organisations.

5. Which man is regarded by many people as the greatest playwright of all time?

    A William Shakespeare

    B Sir Francis Drake

    C Thomas Hardy

    D Charles Dickens

6. At what age can you drink wine or beer with a meal in a hotel or restaurant, as long as you are with someone who is over 18?

    A 14

    B 16

    C 18

    D 21

7. When were women over the age of 30 given voting rights?

    A 1870

    B 1918

    C 1928

    D 1969

8. Which of the following must be displayed in your car?

    A Your driving licence

    B A certificate of insurance

    C A road tax disc

    D An MOT certificate

Practice Test 15

9. Approximately how many British casualties were there in the First World War?

   A 10,000
   B 100,000
   C 2 million
   D 10 million

10. Which of the following Formula 1 World Championship winners is NOT British?

   A Damon Hill
   B Sebastian Vettel
   C Jenson Button
   D Lewis Hamilton

11. Is the statement below true or false?
    'William Beveridge was the author of the Beveridge Report, which introduced free secondary education in England and Wales.'

   A TRUE
   B FALSE

12. Who elected the Police and Crime Commissioners in 2012?

   A The general public
   B The House of Commons
   C The House of Lords
   D The cabinet

13. Is the statement below true or false?
    'The official name of the UK is the United Kingdom of Great Britain.'

   A TRUE
   B FALSE

14. Which of these statements is correct?

   A In AD 43 Britain was successfully invaded by the Romans under Julius Caesar.
   B In AD 43 Britain was successfully invaded by the Romans under the Emperor Claudius.

15. Which of these statements is correct?

   A The Mercury Music Prize is awarded each September for the best album from the UK and Ireland.
   B The Mercury Music Prize is awarded each September for the best live album from Europe.

16. Which TWO of the following are funded by National Insurance Contributions?

   A The police
   B The armed forces
   C The state retirement pension
   D The National Health Service

Practice Test 15

17. Which TWO of the following were included in the three Estates of the early Scottish Parliament?

A   The peasants

B   The clergy

C   The commons

D   The middle classes

18. At which TWO types of election can an MP be elected?

A   Local authority elections

B   By-elections

C   European elections

D   General Elections

19. Is the statement below true or false?
'The English language has many accents and dialects.'

A   TRUE

B   FALSE

20. Is the statement below true or false?
'Queen Victoria reigned for almost 46 years.'

A   TRUE

B   FALSE

21. Is the statement below true or false?
'Schools are not permitted to organise events to raise money for extra equipment or out-of-school activities.'

A   TRUE

B   FALSE

22. Bank notes in the UK come in denominations (values) of £5, £10, £20 and

A   £30

B   £50

C   £150

D   £250

23. When James II returned to challenge William and Mary for the throne, he was defeated at the Battle of the Boyne in

A   Ireland

B   Scotland

C   Dorset

D   Wales

24. Which TWO of the following are members of the cabinet?

A   The Home Secretary

B   The leader of the opposition

C   The Speaker

D   The Chancellor of the Exchequer

Practice Test 16

1. Which TWO are poets who wrote during the Middle Ages?

   A   William Blake
   B   Lord Byron
   C   Geoffrey Chaucer
   D   John Barbour

2. Which of these statements is correct?

   A   When married couples have children, both parents are equally responsible for their children.
   B   When married couples have children, the mother is solely responsible for their children.

3. Is the statement below true or false?
   'The monarch is forbidden from advising the Prime Minister.'

   A   TRUE
   B   FALSE

4. Which of these statements is correct?

   A   Between 1680 and 1720, many refugees called Huguenots came to Britain to escape religious persecution.
   B   Between 1680 and 1720, many refugees called Huguenots came to Britain to escape famine.

5. Is the statement below true or false?
   'As part of the citizenship ceremony, new citizens must pledge to give their loyalty to the United Kingdom.'

   A   TRUE
   B   FALSE

6. Is the statement below true or false?
   'Queen Mary was a devout Catholic and became known as 'Bloody Mary' because of her persecution of Protestants.'

   A   TRUE
   B   FALSE

7. Which of these statements is correct?

   A   It is not illegal to take a woman abroad for female genital mutilation.
   B   It is illegal to take a woman abroad for female genital mutilation.

8. Government services such as roads, education and the police are paid for by

   A   lottery funds
   B   government-owned banks
   C   National Insurance Contributions
   D   income tax

Practice Test 16

9. Which of the following statements is correct?

   A Bonnie Prince Charlie and his Scottish supporters were defeated by George II at the Battle of Culloden.

   B Bonnie Prince Charlie and his Scottish supporters were defeated by George II at the Battle of the Boyne.

10. Which TWO languages are used in the National Assembly for Wales?

    A English
    B Gaelic
    C Welsh
    D Cornish

11. Is the statement below true or false?
    'Isambard Kingdom Brunel built tunnels, railway lines, ships and bridges, including the Clifton Suspension Bridge.'

    A TRUE
    B FALSE

12. In which UK country are the cities of Dundee, Glasgow and Aberdeen?

    A Wales
    B Northern Ireland
    C England
    D Scotland

13. The first Archbishop of Canterbury was

    A St Augustine
    B St Columba
    C St Patrick
    D St George

14. Which of the following is usually a responsibility of a Police Community Support Officer?

    A Giving first aid at crime scenes
    B Patrolling the streets
    C Cleaning up graffiti and vandalism
    D Working with prisoners

15. Wimbledon, the oldest tennis tournament in the world, is the only 'Grand Slam' played on

    A clay courts
    B grass courts
    C hard courts
    D carpet courts

16. Which TWO of the following battles were fought during the English Civil War?

    A The Battle of Marston Moor
    B The Battle of Bannockburn
    C The Battle of Naseby
    D The Battle of Agincourt

17. The Chancellor of the Exchequer is responsible for

 A the economy
 B crime, policing and immigration
 C health
 D education

18. Gilbert and Sullivan wrote which TWO of the following operas?

 A Carmen
 B The Pirates of Penzance
 C Evita
 D The Mikado

19. Which of these statements is correct?

 A The Turing machine was influential in the development of the modern-day television.
 B The Turing machine was influential in the development of the modern-day computer.

20. Which TWO groups of people celebrate the religious festival of Diwali?

 A Christians
 B Sikhs
 C Hindus
 D Jews

21. Is the statement below true or false?
'Voting is done in public and anyone can see which candidate you vote for.'

 A TRUE
 B FALSE

22. Is the statement below true or false?
'There are more women than men at university.'

 A TRUE
 B FALSE

23. Which of the following was NOT an ally of Britain during the Second World War?

 A France
 B Australia
 C Canada
 D Japan

24. How many people sit on a jury in Wales?

 A 8
 B 12
 C 6
 D 20

Practice Test 17

1. Which of these statements is correct?

    A   The Scotsman John Logie Baird developed the television in the 1920s.

    B   The Scotsman John Logie Baird developed the television in the 1950s.

2. Which TWO of the following cities are in England?

    A   Aberdeen

    B   Liverpool

    C   Newcastle Upon Tyne

    D   Newport

3. Drivers may use their driving licence until they are

    A   60

    B   65

    C   70

    D   80

4. Is the statement below true or false?
   'The North Atlantic Treaty Organisation (NATO) was set up to resist the perceived threat of invasion by Japan and its allies.'

    A   TRUE

    B   FALSE

5. The Prime Minister has a country house outside London called

    A   Windsor Castle

    B   Buckingham Palace

    C   Chequers

    D   10 Downing Street

6. Is the statement below true or false?
   'Films were first shown publicly in the UK in 1876.'

    A   TRUE

    B   FALSE

7. Which of these statements is correct?

    A   During the reign of James I, Ireland was an almost completely Protestant country.

    B   During the reign of James I, Ireland was an almost completely Catholic country.

8. What does NSPCC stand for?

    A   National Society for the Prevention of Cruelty to Children

    B   National Society for the Protection of Carers and Children

    C   National Society for the Preservation of Churches and Chapels

    D   National Society for the Prevention of Cancer in Children

Practice Test 17

9. Which of the following is NOT one of the freedoms shared by everyone living in the UK?

   A Freedom of belief and religion

   B Freedom of speech

   C A right to join in the election of a government

   D A right to avoid paying tax

10. Which of these statements is correct?

    A Eid al-Fitr celebrates the end of Ramadan, when Muslims have fasted for a week.

    B Eid al-Fitr celebrates the end of Ramadan, when Muslims have fasted for a month.

11. Which TWO of the following did Britain fight against during the First World War?

    A Germany

    B The Austro-Hungarian Empire

    C France

    D The United States

12. Which of the following is NOT a British architect?

    A Sir Edwin Lutyens

    B Sir Christopher Wren

    C Thomas Gainsborough

    D Robert Adam

13. Which of these statements is correct?

    A In the UK, violence in the home is not always a serious crime.

    B In the UK, violence in the home is a serious crime under all circumstances.

14. Is the statement below true or false?
    'Queen Anne had no surviving children, which created uncertainty over the succession to the throne.'

    A TRUE

    B FALSE

15. Is the statement below true or false?
    'The name of anyone accused of a crime can be published in the press.'

    A TRUE

    B FALSE

16. Who was the first king of the House of Tudor?

    A Henry II

    B Henry V

    C Henry VII

    D Henry VIII

17. Which of these statements is correct?

  A Sir Chris Hoy is a Scottish distance runner who has won six Olympic gold medals.

  B Sir Chris Hoy is a Scottish cyclist who has won six Olympic gold medals.

18. Is the statement below true or false?
'Alcohol cannot be bought from a shop by anyone under the age of 21.'

  A TRUE

  B FALSE

19. Which TWO of the following people were prominent writers in the inter-war period?

  A Emmeline Pankhurst

  B Graham Greene

  C Charles Dickens

  D Evelyn Waugh

20. Members of the Northern Ireland Assembly are known as MLAs, which stands for

  A Members of the Legal Assembly

  B Members of the Legislative Association

  C Members of the Lower Assembly

  D Members of the Legislative Assembly

21. Which country has the smallest population?

  A Northern Ireland

  B Wales

  C England

  D Scotland

22. Is the statement below true or false?
'During the 18th century, tea and spices were imported to Britain from North America.'

  A TRUE

  B FALSE

23. Who is the ceremonial head of the Commonwealth?

  A The Queen

  B The Prime Minister

  C The UK government

  D The head of the UK diplomatic service

24. Which TWO are associated with the Battle of Hastings?

  A Harold, the Saxon king of England

  B The Duke of Wellington

  C William, the Duke of Normandy

  D Mary, Queen of Scots

Practice Test 18

1. Is the statement below true or false?
   'Donated blood is used by hospitals to help people who are injured or ill.'

   A TRUE

   B FALSE

2. Which of these statements is correct?

   A Sutton Hoo, in Suffolk, is the burial place of an Anglo-Saxon king.

   B Sutton Hoo, in Suffolk, is the burial place of a Roman emperor.

3. Is the statement below true or false?
   'The shadow cabinet is made up of senior opposition MPs.'

   A TRUE

   B FALSE

4. When is a by-election held?

   A When the Prime Minister decides

   B When an MP dies or resigns

   C When the head of state decides

   D When a previous election has ended in a tie

5. The Wars of the Roses ended in 1485 with the death of King

   A Henry VII

   B Richard III

   C Henry V

   D John

6. Which TWO countries have their patron saint's day as a public holiday?

   A England

   B Northern Ireland

   C Scotland

   D Wales

7. Which building, rebuilt after the great fire of London in 1666, was designed by Sir Christopher Wren?

   A St Paul's Cathedral

   B Westminster Abbey

   C The Houses of Parliament

   D Tower Bridge

8. In which country in the UK do trials for serious crimes take place in a Sheriff Court?

   A England

   B Wales

   C Scotland

   D Northern Ireland

9. Which of these statements is correct?

A On April Fool's Day people play jokes on each other until midday.

B On April Fool's Day people often dress up in frightening costumes to play 'trick or treat'.

10. Is the statement below true or false?
'During the 19th century, the UK produced almost one quarter of the world's iron, coal and cotton cloth.'

A TRUE
B FALSE

11. When could you talk to an MP in person about an issue that concerns you?

A Never
B Every day at their constituency office
C At the House of Lords
D At local surgeries

12. What did the suffragettes campaign for?

A To allow refugees to come to Britain
B The right to join the war effort
C Free education for their children
D The right for women to vote

13. Cardiff is the capital of which country in the UK?

A England
B Scotland
C Wales
D Northern Ireland

14. Which TWO of the following are former Prime Ministers of the UK?

A John Major
B John Constable
C Tony Blair
D Sir Arthur Conan Doyle

15. Is the statement below true or false?
'Baroness Tanni Grey-Thompson has won 16 Paralympic medals and won the London Marathon six times.'

A TRUE
B FALSE

16. In the UK, it is a criminal offence to

A harass someone because of their ethnic origin
B sell tobacco to anyone under the age of 21
C park a car on the street
D own a dog without a licence

17. Which of these statements is correct?

    A The Book of Common Prayer was written to be used in the Church of England.

    B The Book of Common Prayer was written to be used in the Catholic Church.

18. Which TWO of the following are part of 'Great Britain'?

    A England

    B Northern Ireland

    C Isle of Man

    D Wales

19. Which TWO of the following cannot stand for public office in the UK?

    A Pregnant women

    B Members of the armed forces

    C Civil servants

    D Teachers

20. Is the statement below true or false?
'By 1200, the English ruled an area of land in Ireland called the Pale.'

    A TRUE

    B FALSE

21. Which of these statements is correct?

    A In the UK, smoking is not allowed in nearly every enclosed public space.

    B In the UK, smoking is allowed in nearly every enclosed public space.

22. Is the statement below true or false?
'Jane Austen's novels, including 'Oliver Twist' and 'Great Expectations', are concerned with marriage and family relationships.'

    A TRUE

    B FALSE

23. Is the statement below true or false?
'People in the UK have to pay income tax on income from property and savings.'

    A TRUE

    B FALSE

24. Which Conservative MP oversaw the introduction of the Education Act 1944, which introduced free secondary education in England and Wales?

    A R A Butler

    B Clement Attlee

    C Margaret Thatcher

    D Dylan Thomas

Practice Test 19

1. Which TWO of the following groups of people migrated to Britain in the 17th and 18th centuries?

    A Saxons

    B Jews

    C Huguenots

    D Jutes

2. Which of these statements is correct?

    A Lucian Freud, a French-born British artist, is best known for his portraits.

    B Lucian Freud, a German-born British artist, is best known for his portraits.

3. What plate must a newly qualified driver display in Northern Ireland?

    A L Plate

    B D Plate

    C R Plate

    D P Plate

4. Which of these statements is correct?

    A The Battle of Trafalgar was fought by the British navy against the combined French and German fleets.

    B The Battle of Trafalgar was fought by the British navy against the combined French and Spanish fleets.

5. The Ashes is a series of matches played between England and Australia in which sport?

    A Rugby

    B Cricket

    C Hockey

    D Basketball

6. Is the statement below true or false?
    'Initially the Normans also conquered Scotland, but the Scots gradually won their territory back.'

    A TRUE

    B FALSE

7. Which of the following is not part of the UK?

    A Scotland

    B Wales

    C Northern Ireland

    D The Channel Islands

8. Is the statement below true or false?
    'Taxation is under the control of the devolved administration in Wales.'

    A TRUE

    B FALSE

Practice Test 19

9. Where would you find the Stone Age site of Skara Brae?

   A   In Wiltshire
   B   On Orkney
   C   In Edinburgh
   D   On Shetland

10. The National Eisteddfod is an annual cultural festival including music, dance and art, held in

   A   Wales
   B   Scotland
   C   England
   D   Northern Ireland

11. Is the statement below true or false?
'The 'Highland Clearances' were where Scottish landlords evicted people on small farms to make way for sheep and cattle.'

   A   TRUE
   B   FALSE

12. Which TWO of the following flowers are particularly associated with UK countries?

   A   Tulip
   B   Rose
   C   Lily
   D   Daffodil

13. Which TWO of the following are major political parties in the UK?

   A   The Green Party
   B   The Labour Party
   C   The Conservative Party
   D   The Democratic Party

14. Which of these statements is correct?

   A   The Battle of Agincourt in 1415 was one of the most famous battles of the Wars of the Roses.
   B   The Battle of Agincourt in 1415 was one of the most famous battles of the Hundred Years War.

15. Is the statement below true or false?
'The modern Scottish Parliament was formed in 1999.'

   A   TRUE
   B   FALSE

16. Which TWO of the following are novels by Thomas Hardy?

   A   Treasure Island
   B   Brighton Rock
   C   Far from the Madding Crowd
   D   Jude the Obscure

Practice Test 19

17. Most member states of the Commonwealth were once part of

A   the Council of Europe

B   the United Nations

C   the European Union

D   the British Empire

18. Which of these statements is correct?

A   Henry VII was thrifty and built up the monarchy's financial reserves.

B   Henry VII spent the monarchy's financial reserves on building great castles.

19. Is the statement below true or false?

'All dogs in public places must wear a collar showing the name and date of birth of the owner.'

A   TRUE

B   FALSE

20. Is the statement below true or false?

'The playwright William Shakespeare focused solely on kings and queens in his play.'

A   TRUE

B   FALSE

21. Which of these statements is correct?

A   A woman's husband can be charged with rape if he forces her to have sex with him.

B   A woman's husband cannot be charged with rape if he forces her to have sex with him.

22. Which festival, in November or December, remembers the Jews' struggle for religious freedom?

A   Hannukah

B   Eid al-Fitr

C   Vaisakhi

D   Christmas

23. Which of the following people was voted the greatest Briton of all time in 2002?

A   Sir Robert Walpole

B   Winston Churchill

C   Graham Greene

D   Clement Attlee

24. Is the statement below true or false?

'The laws and conventions of Britain are written down in a document called the British Constitution.'

A   TRUE

B   FALSE

Practice Test 20

1. Is the statement below true or false?
   'Everyone living in the UK should respect and support the fundamental values and principles of British society.'

   A   TRUE
   B   FALSE

2. The Saxon king of England, who was defeated at the Battle of Hastings, was called

   A   Henry I
   B   Alfred the Great
   C   Harold
   D   Kenneth MacAlpin

3. Which of these statements is correct?

   A   On Valentine's Day children send cards or buy gifts for their mothers.
   B   On Valentine's Day lovers exchange cards and gifts.

4. If you are resident in the UK, which TWO of the following must you have for your car?

   A   Breakdown cover
   B   A road tax disc
   C   Air conditioning
   D   Valid motor insurance

5. To divorce his first wife, Catherine of Aragon, Henry VIII needed approval from

   A   the Archbishop of Canterbury
   B   the King of Spain
   C   the Pope
   D   Parliament

6. Who wrote 'Land of Hope and Glory', which is usually played at the Last Night of the Proms at the Royal Albert Hall?

   A   Sir Edward Elgar
   B   Henry Purcell
   C   Benjamin Britten
   D   Paul McCartney

7. Which of these statements is correct?

   A   Charles II established the Royal Society to promote 'natural knowledge'.
   B   Charles II established the Royal Society to promote the arts.

8. The second-largest party in the House of Commons is called the

   A   civil service
   B   judiciary
   C   cabinet
   D   opposition

9. During the Second World War, who defeated the British in Singapore and then occupied Burma?

   A Japan
   B India
   C Russia
   D China

10. Who is the chairperson of the General Assembly of the Church of Scotland?

    A The monarch
    B The Archbishop of Canterbury
    C The Pope
    D The Moderator

11. Who is responsible for appointing the local Chief Constable?

    A The general public
    B The police force
    C The local MP
    D The Police and Crime Commissioner

12. The Magna Carta (Great Charter) was a charter of rights introduced in

    A 1066
    B 1100
    C 1215
    D 1348

13. Is the statement below true or false?
    'Andrew Lloyd Webber and Tim Rice have collaborated on shows including 'The Mikado' and 'HMS Pinafore'.'

    A TRUE
    B FALSE

14. Is the statement below true or false?
    'The Industrial Revolution happened because of the development of machinery and the use of steam power.'

    A TRUE
    B FALSE

15. Which TWO are features of the small claims procedure?

    A The hearing is in front of a judge
    B Cases are heard in the Crown Court
    C There is a jury
    D Cases are heard in an ordinary room

16. If you watch TV, but are not covered by a TV licence, then you may face

    A a fine
    B imprisonment
    C the confiscation of your TV
    D a rise in the cost of your TV licence

Practice Test 20

17. Is the statement below true or false?
'Until 1870, when a woman got married, her earnings, property and money belonged to her husband.'

- **A** TRUE
- **B** FALSE

18. Which TWO events did the distance runner Mo Farah win gold medals in during the 2012 Olympic Games?

- **A** 400 metres
- **B** 5,000 metres
- **C** 10,000 metres
- **D** Marathon

19. Is the statement below true or false?
'The National Assembly for Wales needs the agreement of the UK Parliament to pass laws about housing in Wales.'

- **A** TRUE
- **B** FALSE

20. Which of these statements is correct?

- **A** 'Home Rule' for Ireland meant Ireland would remain in the UK but have its own parliament.
- **B** 'Home Rule' for Ireland meant Ireland would be completely independent from the UK.

21. Is the statement below true or false?
'The House of Commons has powers to overrule the House of Lords, and these are often used.'

- **A** TRUE
- **B** FALSE

22. Which of these statements is correct?

- **A** Wales has its own bank notes which are valid everywhere in the UK.
- **B** Scotland has its own bank notes which are valid everywhere in the UK.

23. Which TWO of the following charities work to protect the environment?

- **A** Crisis
- **B** Friends of the Earth
- **C** NSPCC
- **D** The National Trust

24. What is the name of the supersonic passenger aircraft developed in Britain and France?

- **A** Harrier
- **B** Spitfire
- **C** Hurricane
- **D** Concorde

Answers

Practice Test 1

1. B
2. A
3. B — Tip: Only Scotland and Northern Ireland have their patron saint's day as an official holiday (although in Scotland not all businesses and offices will close).
4. B — Tip: In the late 1970s, imports were valued at more than the price paid for exports.
5. B — Tip: The London Eye was built as part of the UK's celebrations of the new millennium.
6. B
7. C
8. B
9. A
10. A, B
11. A, B
12. A
13. C, D
14. D — Tip: Using public transport produces less pollution than driving a car.
15. A
16. A
17. B — Tip: The jury decides whether the defendant is guilty or not guilty, and the judge decides the penalty.
18. B, D
19. B
20. A
21. A
22. D
23. B, C
24. B

Practice Test 2

1. B
2. B — Tip: Elections to the Scottish Parliament and the National Assembly for Wales use a form of proportional representation.
3. A
4. A, C
5. B — Tip: During the First World War, Germany, the Austro-Hungarian Empire and the Ottoman Empire were the main Central Powers.
6. A, B
7. A, C
8. A
9. D
10. A
11. A
12. B
13. C
14. B — Tip: Jayne Torvill and Christopher Dean won gold medals at the 1984 Olympic Games for ice dancing.
15. A, D
16. A
17. B
18. B — Tip: The Falkland Islands are a British overseas territory in the South Atlantic Ocean.
19. B — Tip: Charles II was succeeded by his brother because he had no legitimate children.
20. B
21. D
22. B
23. A
24. D

Answers

Practice Test 3

1. B
2. B
3. D
4. B — Tip: John Maynard Keynes published influential new theories of economics.
5. A, C
6. A
7. A, C
8. C
9. B
10. A
11. B — Tip: The first professional football clubs in the UK were formed in the late 19th century.
12. A
13. A
14. B — Tip: It was Emperor Hadrian who built a wall to keep out the Picts. It is called Hadrian's Wall.
15. A, B
16. B — Tip: Parliament passed the laws giving women the right to equal pay in the 1960s.
17. A, D
18. B
19. B — Tip: London's West End is often known as 'Theatreland'.
20. C
21. B
22. B
23. B
24. A — Tip: Complaints can be made to the Independent Police Complaints Commission, but they can also be made at your local police station.

Practice Test 4

1. A
2. B, C
3. C
4. A
5. D
6. B — Tip: There is no place in UK society for extremism or intolerance.
7. C
8. C
9. A, C
10. B — Tip: Admiral Nelson was in charge of the British fleet at the Battle of Trafalgar in 1805, and was killed in the battle.
11. B, C
12. C
13. B — Tip: In 2012, the cyclist Bradley Wiggins became the first Briton to win the Tour de France.
14. B
15. B
16. D
17. B — Tip: Parents often help in schools, for example by listening to children read.
18. A
19. B — Tip: Using recycled materials to make new products reduces the amount of rubbish being put into landfill.
20. B — Tip: The Archbishop of Canterbury can be selected by the monarch, but is usually selected by the Prime Minister and a committee appointed by the Church.
21. A, D
22. B
23. A
24. D

Answers

Practice Test 5

1. D
2. D
3. A
4. A
5. A
6. A — Tip: In the Middle Ages, knights and wealthy people from towns and cities were elected to sit in the House of Commons.
7. B
8. A
9. B — Tip: During the 1950s, there was a shortage of labour — this means that there were lots of jobs, but there were not enough people to do them.
10. D
11. A
12. B
13. B — Tip: 'Pocket boroughs' were constituencies controlled by a single wealthy family.
14. C
15. C, D
16. A
17. A
18. D
19. A — Tip: According to the 2009 Citizenship Survey, 4% of people in the UK are Muslim and less than 0.5% are Jewish.
20. B
21. B, C — Tip: The fundamental principles of British life also include democracy, individual liberty and tolerance of those with different faiths and beliefs.
22. A
23. B, D
24. D

Practice Test 6

1. B — Tip: Howard Florey and Ernst Chain developed penicillin into a usable drug after it had been discovered by Alexander Fleming.
2. B
3. B — Tip: The European Union was originally called the European Economic Community (EEC).
4. A
5. C
6. A, D
7. C — Tip: St Helena is a British overseas territory in the Atlantic Ocean.
8. A, D
9. B — Tip: The 'gothic' style became popular again in the 19th century. In the 18th century, simpler designs became popular.
10. C
11. B
12. B — Tip: Sir Robert Walpole was the first man to be known as Prime Minister.
13. A
14. A
15. B
16. B
17. B
18. C, D
19. C
20. B
21. A, B
22. A
23. B — Tip: The Home Secretary is responsible for crime, policing and immigration. The Chancellor of the Exchequer is responsible for the country's economy.
24. B — Tip: 'EastEnders' and 'Coronation Street' are examples of television soap operas.

Answers

Practice Test 7

1. D
2. A
3. B, D
4. A, B
5. B
6. A
7. A
8. A
9. A
10. C
11. B
12. A, B
13. C — Tip: Treating others with fairness is one of the responsibilities of being a British citizen.
14. B — Tip: Northern Irish and Scottish bank notes are valid everywhere in the UK.
15. A
16. B
17. A
18. C
19. A
20. B — Tip: Tax is automatically taken from most people's earnings by their employer and is paid directly to HM Revenue and Customs. People who are self-employed need to pay tax through a system called self-assessment.
21. A
22. B
23. A
24. A

Practice Test 8

1. A
2. B, C
3. A, D
4. A, D
5. B
6. B
7. D
8. B — Tip: Stormont, in Belfast, is where the Northern Ireland Assembly meets.
9. A
10. B
11. A
12. C
13. B — Tip: The Battle of Hastings was in 1066.
14. D
15. A, C — Tip: Maiden Castle is an Iron Age hill fort in Dorset. Sutton Hoo, in Suffolk, is the burial place of an Anglo-Saxon king.
16. B — Tip: Magistrates decide the verdict of each case that comes before them and, if the person is found guilty, the sentence that they are given.
17. B
18. B
19. C
20. A
21. A
22. B
23. B
24. B

Answers

Practice Test 9

1. B
2. A, B
3. B
4. B — Tip: Prince Charles is the Prince of Wales and the heir to the throne.
5. B
6. A
7. A, B
8. A
9. D
10. A, D
11. B
12. B — Tip: The Reform Act of 1832 increased the number of people who could vote, but voting was still based on the ownership of property, which meant that the working classes still could not vote.
13. A, D
14. D
15. B
16. A
17. A
18. B — Tip: Education and the armed forces are paid for by income tax.
19. D
20. C
21. A
22. B — Tip: The Speaker is an MP, but is neutral and does not represent a political party.
23. B — Tip: The first Christian communities began to appear in Britain during the 3rd and 4th centuries AD.
24. C

Practice Test 10

1. B
2. A
3. B, D
4. A
5. A — Tip: Carding is the process of preparing fibres for spinning into yarn.
6. B, D
7. B
8. A
9. B
10. A
11. A, C
12. D
13. C
14. A
15. A
16. A, C
17. A
18. C
19. A
20. A
21. D
22. A, B
23. B
24. B — Tip: Holman Hunt, Dante Gabriel Rossetti and Sir John Millais were part of an important group of artists known as the Pre-Raphaelites.

Answers

Practice Test 11

1. B — Tip: On Valentine's Day, people send anonymous cards to someone they secretly admire.
2. B, C
3. A
4. B
5. B — Tip: MPs are elected through a system called 'first past the post'.
6. A
7. C, D
8. B
9. A
10. A — Tip: John O'Groats is on the north coast of Scotland.
11. A
12. A
13. B
14. B, C
15. A
16. B, C
17. D
18. B
19. A — Tip: In the Bronze Age, people made weapons, ornaments and tools out of bronze. In the Iron Age, people made weapons and tools out of iron.
20. B
21. B
22. B
23. B — Tip: When Henry VII died he was succeeded by his son Henry VIII.
24. C

Practice Test 12

1. B
2. C
3. A
4. A
5. B, C
6. D
7. C
8. D
9. A
10. A
11. A, C
12. A
13. B
14. B — Tip: 'Lucky Jim' was written by the novelist and poet Sir Kingsley Amis.
15. B — Tip: Voluntary work benefits the community, for example by volunteering in a litter pick-up you will improve the environment of the local area.
16. B
17. B — Tip: A hearing in a small claims procedure is held in front of a judge in an ordinary room.
18. B — Tip: Protestant ideas gradually gained strength in England, Wales and Scotland during the 16th century.
19. B — Tip: Since 1999, hereditary peers have lost the automatic right to attend the House of Lords.
20. D
21. A
22. A, C
23. B
24. A, C

Answers

Practice Test 13

1. B — Tip: More women than men study at university in the UK.
2. B — Tip: Citizens of the UK have a responsibility to look after themselves, their family and the area they live in.
3. B, C
4. B — Tip: When the Queen opens a parliamentary session, she gives a speech summarising the government's policies for the year ahead.
5. B, D
6. B, C
7. A
8. C
9. A, D
10. A
11. D
12. B — Tip: The first ATM was put into use in 1967.
13. D — Tip: Drivers with a licence from the EU, Norway and Liechtenstein may drive in the UK for the duration of their licence. Drivers from any other country may drive for 12 months, before they need a UK full driving licence.
14. B
15. A, D
16. A
17. A
18. B — Tip: St Patrick's day is on 17 March and St Andrew's day is on 30 November.
19. A
20. B
21. B
22. A
23. B
24. B

Practice Test 14

1. B
2. B — Tip: Criminal law relates to crimes. Civil law is used to settle disputes between individuals or groups.
3. B
4. C
5. D
6. B — Tip: Arranged marriage (where both people agree to the marriage) is legal in the UK.
7. A
8. B — Tip: The 40 days before Easter are known as Lent.
9. B
10. D
11. B
12. A — Tip: Ireland was an almost completely Catholic country at this time and there were a number of rebellions against Protestant English rule.
13. B — Tip: People aged over 75 can apply for a free TV licence.
14. C
15. A, C
16. B, C
17. B
18. C
19. A
20. C
21. B
22. A, C
23. C, D
24. A

Answers

Practice Test 15

1. A
2. A
3. B
4. B
5. A
6. B
7. B
8. C
9. C
10. B
11. B — Tip: The Beveridge Report provided the basis for the modern welfare state. The Butler Act introduced free secondary education in England and Wales.
12. A
13. B — Tip: The official name of the UK is the United Kingdom of Great Britain and Northern Ireland.
14. B
15. A
16. C, D
17. B, C
18. B, D
19. A
20. B — Tip: Queen Victoria reigned for almost 64 years.
21. B
22. B
23. A
24. A, D

Practice Test 16

1. C, D
2. A
3. B — Tip: The monarch can advise, warn and encourage the Prime Minister.
4. A — Tip: Irish people came to Britain to escape famine in the 19th Century.
5. A
6. A
7. B
8. D
9. A
10. A, C
11. A
12. D
13. A
14. B
15. B
16. A, C
17. A
18. B, D
19. B
20. B, C
21. B
22. A
23. D
24. B

Answers

Practice Test 17

1. A
2. B, C
3. C
4. B — Tip: NATO was set up to resist the perceived threat of invasion by the Soviet Union and its allies.
5. C
6. B — Tip: Films were first shown publicly in the UK in 1896.
7. B
8. A
9. D
10. B
11. A, B
12. C — Tip: Thomas Gainsborough was an artist.
13. B
14. A
15. B — Tip: The names of accused young people under the age of 17 cannot be used by the media.
16. C
17. B
18. B — Tip: Alcohol cannot be bought from a shop by anyone under the age of 18.
19. B, D
20. D
21. A
22. B — Tip: Tea and spices were imported from India and the area that is now called Indonesia.
23. A
24. A, C

Practice Test 18

1. A
2. A
3. A
4. B
5. B
6. B, C
7. A
8. C
9. A
10. B — Tip: During the 19th century, the UK produced more than half of the world's iron, coal and cotton cloth.
11. D — Tip: Many MPs hold local surgeries in their constituencies, where members of the public can come and talk to them in person.
12. D
13. C
14. A, C
15. A
16. A
17. A
18. A, D
19. B, C
20. A
21. A
22. B — Tip: 'Oliver Twist' and 'Great Expectations' are novels by Charles Dickens. Novels by Jane Austen include 'Pride and Prejudice' and 'Sense and Sensibility.'
23. A
24. A

Answers

Practice Test 19

1. B, C
2. B
3. C
4. B
5. B
6. B — Tip: The Normans initially conquered Wales, but never invaded Scotland.
7. D — Tip: The Channel Islands are closely linked to the UK, but they are not part of it.
8. B — Tip: Many public services are now under the control of the devolved administration in Wales, but taxation is not.
9. B
10. A
11. A
12. B, D
13. B, C — Tip: The Liberal Democrats are also a major political party in the UK.
14. B
15. A
16. C, D
17. D
18. A
19. B — Tip: All dogs in public places must wear a collar showing the name and address of the owner.
20. B — Tip: William Shakespeare was one of the first playwrights to portray ordinary Englishmen and women.
21. A — Tip: In the UK any man who forces a woman to have sex with him can be charged with rape, no matter what relationship he has with her.
22. A
23. B
24. B — Tip: The British Constitution is not written down in any single document.

Practice Test 20

1. A
2. C
3. B
4. B, D
5. C
6. A
7. A
8. D
9. A
10. D
11. D
12. C
13. B — Tip: 'The Mikado' and 'HMS Pinafore' are comic operas by Gilbert and Sullivan.
14. A
15. A, D
16. A
17. A — Tip: Acts of Parliament in 1870 and 1882 gave wives the right to keep their own earnings and property.
18. B, C
19. B — Tip: Since 2011 the National Assembly for Wales has been able to pass laws on education, health and social services, economic development and housing without the agreement of the UK Parliament.
20. A
21. B — Tip: The House of Commons does not often use its powers to overrule the House of Lords.
22. B
23. B, D
24. D

Glossary

The important words that have been used in this book are explained in this glossary.

To help you understand some of the more difficult words, some explanations are followed by an example of how the word could be used.

A few entries are followed by a word in brackets, such as arrested (police). This tells you the context the word is being used in.

Different definitions are separated by a slash (/).

AD	Anno Domini — referring to the number of years after the birth of Jesus Christ — used as a time reference.
allegiance	Loyalty to something — for example, to a leader, a faith or a country.
armed forces	The army, navy and air force which defend a country in times of peace and war.
arrested (police)	Taken by the police to a police station and made to stay there to answer questions about illegal actions or activity.
assault	The criminal act of using physical force against someone or of attacking someone — for example, hitting someone.
bank holiday	A day when most people have an official day off work and many businesses are closed. A bank holiday can also be called a public holiday.
baron	A man who has one of the ranks of the British nobility. The title was particularly common during the Middle Ages.
BC	Before Christ — referring to the number of years before Jesus Christ was born — used as a time reference.
bishop	A senior member of the clergy in the Christian religion, often in charge of the churches in a particular area.
boom	A sharp rise in something — very often in business activity or the economy.

brutality	Behaviour towards another which is cruel and violent and causes harm.
by-election	An election held in a parliamentary constituency or local authority area to fill a vacancy (*see also* General Election).
cabinet (government)	A group of senior ministers who are responsible for controlling government policy.
casualties (medical)	People who are wounded or killed (for example, in a war).
charter (government)	An official written statement which describes the rights and responsibilities of a state and its citizens.
chieftain	The leader of a clan in Scotland or Ireland.
civil disobedience	The refusal of members of the public to obey laws, often because they want to protest against political issues.
civil law	The legal system that deals with disputes between people or groups of people.
civil service	The departments within the government which manage the business of running the country — people who work for the government can be called civil servants.
civil war	A war between groups who live in the same country.
clan	A group of people or families who live under the rule of a chieftain and may be descendants of the same person — a term used traditionally in Scotland.
clergy	Religious leaders, used here to describe religious leaders in Christian churches.
coalition	A partnership between different political parties.
colonise	Inhabit and take control of another country. People who colonise are called colonists.
commemorate	Show that something or someone is remembered.
conquered	Beaten in battle.

constituency	A specific area where the voters who live in that place (its constituents) can elect an MP to represent them in Parliament.
constitution (law)	The legal structure of established laws and principles which is used to govern a country.
convention (government)	An agreement, often between countries, about particular rules or codes of behaviour.
criminal law	The legal system that deals with illegal activities.
decree (law)	Official order, law or decision.
democratic country	A country which is governed by people who are elected by the population to represent them in Parliament.
devolution	The passing of power from a central government to another group at a regional or local level, which can then be called a devolved administration.
dialect	A form of a language spoken by a particular group or people living in a particular area.
domestic policies	Political decisions that relate to what is happening within a country (as opposed to in another country).
electoral register	The official list of all the people in a country who are allowed to vote in an election.
electorate	All the people who are allowed to vote in an election.
eligible	Allowed by law.
ethnic origin	The country of birth, someone's race or the nationality of someone when they were born / the customs and place from which a person and their family originated (or came from).
executed	Killed as a punishment.
first past the post	A system of election in which the candidate with the largest number of votes in a particular constituency wins a seat in Parliament.
franchise	The right to vote.

General Election	An event in which all the citizens of a country who are allowed to vote choose the people they wish to represent them in their government.
government policies	Official ideas and beliefs that are agreed by a political party about how to govern the country.
guilty	Found by a court to have done something which is illegal.
heir	Someone who will legally receive a person's money or possessions after their death. The heir to the throne is the person who will become the next king or queen.
House (history)	A family (for example, House of York).
House of Commons	That part of the Houses of Parliament where MPs who are elected by the voting public debate political issues.
House of Lords	That part of the Houses of Parliament where people who have inherited their place or been chosen by the government debate political issues.
household	A home and the people who live in it / something that relates to a home. (For example, household chores are tasks that are done around the house, such as cleaning and cooking.)
Houses of Parliament	The building in London where the House of Commons and House of Lords meet.
illegal	Something which the law does not allow.
infrastructure	Structured network that is necessary for successful operation of a business or transport system — for example, roads or railways.
innocent (law)	Found by a court not to have done something illegal.
judge	The most important official in court. The judge makes sure what happens in court is fair and legal.
judiciary	All the judges in a country. Together, they are responsible for using the law of the land in the correct way.
jury (legal)	People who are chosen to sit in court, listen to information about a crime, and decide if someone is guilty or innocent.

legal	Allowed to do so by law.
legislative power	The power to make laws.
liberty	Freedom.
magistrate	A person who acts as a judge in a court case where the crime is not a serious one.
marital status	Information about whether a person is single, married, separated or divorced. This is often asked for on official forms.
media, the	All the organisations which give information to the public, i.e. newspapers, magazines, television, radio and the internet.
medieval/Middle Ages	In history, the period between 1066 and about 1500.
monarch	The king or queen of a country.
national issues	Political problems that can affect everyone who lives in a country.
nationalised	Bought and then controlled by central government — relating to an industry or service that was previously owned privately.
nobility	The people in a country who belong to the highest social class, some of whom may have titles — for example, Lord, Duke, Baron.
office, to be in	To be in power in government.
Olympics	International sporting event held every four years.
opposition	In the House of Commons, the largest political party which is not part of the government is officially known as the opposition.
Pale (history)	Part of Ireland governed by the English.
party politics	The shared ideas and beliefs of an organised group of politicians.
patron saint	A Christian saint who is believed to protect a particular area or group of people.
penalty (law)	Punishment for breaking the law.

Pope, the	The head of the Roman Catholic Church.
practise a religion	Live according to the rules and beliefs of a religion.
Prime Minister	The politician who leads the government.
prohibit/prohibition	Make something illegal.
proportional representation	A system of election in which political parties are allowed a number of seats in Parliament that represents their share of the total number of votes cast.
Protestants	Christians who are not members of the Roman Catholic Church.
public body	A governmental department or a group of people who represent or work for the government and who work for the good of the general public.
public house/pub	A place where adults can buy and drink alcohol.
Reformation, the	The religious movement in the 16th century that challenged the authority of the Pope and established Protestant churches in Europe.
refugee	A person who must leave the country where they live, often because of a war or for political reasons.
residence	The place where someone lives.
rival viewpoints	Opinions held by different groups of people.
rural	Countryside.
scrutinise	Examine all the details.
seat (Parliament)	A constituency.
sentence	A punishment imposed by a court.
shadow cabinet	Senior MPs of a political party not in government.
sheriff (law)	A judge in Scotland.
slavery	A system in which people bought and sold other people (slaves) who were forced to work without pay.
sonnet	A poem which is 14 lines long and rhymes in a particular way.
Speaker, the	The member of the House of Commons who controls the way issues are debated in Parliament.

stand for office	Apply to be elected — for example, as an MP or councillor.
strike, to go on	Refuse to work in order to protest against something.
successor (government)	A person who comes after another and takes over an office or receives some kind of power — for example, a son who becomes king when his father dies is his successor.
suspend	To stop something from happening or operating, usually for a short time.
terrorism	Violence used by people who want to force a government to do something. The violence is usually random and unexpected, so that no one can feel really safe from it.
The Phone Book	A book which contains names, addresses and phone numbers of organisations, businesses and individuals.
theft	The criminal act of stealing something from a person, building or place.
trade union	An association of workers formed to protect its members.
treaty	An official written agreement between countries or governments.
uprising	A violent revolt or rebellion against an authority.
voluntary work	Work which someone does because they want to and which they do for free, i.e. they do not receive any payment.
volunteer	Someone who works for free or who offers to do something without payment (see voluntary work).
war effort	The work people did in order to help the country in any way they could during wartime.
Yellow Pages	A book that lists names, addresses and telephone numbers of businesses, services and organisations in an area. Also available online at www.yell.com.

Index

U

V

W

Y

Acknowledgements:

The material in Chapters 1 – 5 marked with quotation marks is crown copyright and has been reproduced from the government publication 'Life in the United Kingdom: A Guide for New Residents' (ISBN 978-0-11-341340-9). This material has been reproduced with the permission of The National Archives under the Open Government Licence — http://www.nationalarchives.gov. uk/doc/open-government-licence/

All other text is copyright of Coordination Group Publications Ltd

With thanks to iStockphoto.com for permission to reproduce the images used on pages 5, 8, 10, 11, 12, 14, 16, 21, 30, 35, 43, 44, 45, 51, 68, 71, 75, 78, 85, 87, 89, 95, 102, 103, 104, 105, 106, 109, 113, 129, 139, 143 and 146.

Cover image © iStockphoto.com / George Paul

With thanks to Getty Images for permission to reproduce the image used on page 13

Page 19: King John signs the Great Charter, Doyle, James E. (19th Century) / Private Collection / © Look and Learn / The Bridgeman Art Library

Page 23: Portrait of Mary I or Mary Tudor (1516-58), daughter of Henry VIII, at the Age of 28, 1544 (panel), Master John (fl.1544) / National Portrait Gallery, London, UK / The Bridgeman Art Library

Page 29: Portrait of Oliver Cromwell (oil on canvas), Lely, Sir Peter (1618-80) / Private Collection / Photo © Christie's Images / The Bridgeman Art Library

Page 36: Robert Burns, after a 19th century print (colour litho), Scottish School, (19th century) / Private Collection / Ken Welsh / The Bridgeman Art Library

Page 47: Portrait of Emmeline Pankhurst (1857-1928) (acrylic on canvas), English School, (20th century) / Private Collection / The Bridgeman Art Library

Page 54: The Victory "V" (photogravure), English Photographer, (20th century) / Private Collection / The Stapleton Collection / The Bridgeman Art Library

With thanks to Rex Features for permission to reproduce the image used on page 65

With thanks to Alamy for permission to reproduce the images used on pages 71 and 100

LUHRA1